Start-Up Money

Raise What You Need for Your Small Business

Jennifer Lindsey

WILEY

John Wiley & Sons

New York • Chichester • Brisbane • Toronto • Singapore

Library of Congress Cataloging in Publication Data:

Lindsey, Jennifer.
    Start-up money : raise what you need for your small business /
Jennifer Lindsey.
        p.   cm.
    Bibliography: p.
    ISBN 0-471-50032-1. — ISBN 0-471-50031-3 (pbk.)
    1. Small business—Finance. 2. Commercial loans. I. Title.
HG4027.7.L56   1989   88-32626
658.1′5224—dc19   CIP

To entrepreneurs
who bet the company and win

Preface

When start-up money got harder to raise in 1987, and more expensive, I decided to write a book for the small business owners who find it hardest of all: the seekers of $100,000 or less in debt or equity capital. Often scorned by commercial bankers, ignored by investment bankers, and frequently broke at the end of two operating years, this market seemed to deserve a book of its own that would put the keys to the cash kingdom at least a little closer to hand.

This book covers the basic financing strategies that can be adapted and used by an entrepreneur to raise small amounts of capital. Many of the techniques have been around for years; some have been, until now, inappropriate for small financings. But with only a slight adjustment, they can be restructured to yield financings as low as $50,000, through business value lending (BVL) for small "sons of leveraged buyouts," for example. In fact, the economy is changing so noticeably that U.S. commercial banks who once shunned small business lending now create BVL departments to handle the overflow demand for this new trend in asset-based lending.

It may seem surprising to find offshore financing sources cited throughout the book. If you own a dress shop on Main Street, the connection between your need for a $50,000 loan and merchant banks in Holland may seem tenuous at best. But consider how the world is shrinking: In some states, more than 50 percent of the retail clothing products for sale are produced in foreign countries. If your dress shop is the world's only outlet for Xenobia sportswear, and the world wants Xenobia sportswear, you'll get a

$75,000 loan and a lot more if you agree to start up a tax-free production facility to manufacture the sportswear in Holland.

The point is, your competitors for market share and available financing will come, increasingly, from offshore businesses located in the United States or overseas. If you do not take advantage of new and newly available financing sources in the face of global competition, your business vision and subsequent growth will be limited by your inability to access the larger capital market.

What has felt like economic chaos to many owners the last two years can mean limitless opportunity for those who make financial moves at the right time. Chapter 1 constitutes a short course on how to read newspaper headlines in a way that makes sense for small business owners. Every tremor in the stock market won't have a direct effect on your business, but a few variables will. Understand how to use those movements and, at the very least, you will be able to plan your financings a little more knowledgeably, raising money more quickly and easily. Many thanks are due the scores of entrepreneurs I have interviewed and worked with over the past eight years, as well as the attorneys, bankers, accountants, investment bankers, and venture capitalists who helped this effort by supplying information, technical overview, and encouragement: Patrick Powell, Broncorp Manufacturing Co., Inc.; Gail W. Sevier and Linda Dreiling, Arthur Young; Charles Friedman, Friedman & Solomon; Steven E. Leatherman, Boettcher & Company; B.J. Rockefeller, Copadco Ltd.; Duane Pearsall, Columbine Venture Fund Ltd.; Karl Dakin, tku Technologies; and John Eckstein, Calkins, Kramer, Grimshaw & Harring.

Contents

Introduction

▶ **Balance of Trade:** The net difference between the value of U.S. imports and exports of merchandise over time. When the U.S. exports or sells more than it imports, it has an advantageous balance of trade. If imports predominate, the balance is not considered advantageous. Influencing factors include the strength of the dollar compared to the currencies of the countries with which the U.S. trades, the level of U.S. manufacturing strength compared worldwide, and the total U.S. economy when production is not meeting demand.

▶ **Business Cycle:** The natural recurrence of corporate expansion (or recovery) and contraction (or recession) in normal business activity, which affects growth, employment, and inflation. It also affects profitability and cash flow, which makes a business cycle a key ingredient in corporate dividend policies, and in the rise and fall of interest rates. A complete business cycle using a gross national product baseline includes one expansion and one contraction over approximately two and one-half years.

▶ **Gross National Product (GNP):** The total value of goods and services produced in the U.S. economy over a one-year period of time, including consumer and government purchases, private, domestic, and foreign investments in the United States, and the total dollar value of U.S. exports. The GNP growth rate is considered the top indicator of America's economic health. GNP figures are released quarterly by the federal government as inflation-adjusted figures, or Real GNP.

▶ **Inflationary:** The tendency toward a rise in the price of goods and services in general, as when spending increases relative to the supply of goods available, or too much money is chasing too few goods. Although moderate inflation is a sign of growth, hyperinflation produces price increases of 100 percent or more every year, which prompts consumers to lose confidence in the dollar and invest in hard assets like gold or real estate.

▶ **Monetary Policy:** Any decision of the Federal Reserve Board (Fed) which affects the nation's money supply. To control the level of economic activity, the Fed can make the economy grow faster by supplying more credit to the banking system through open market operations; or it can lower the member bank reserve requirement or lower the discount rate, which is the rate banks pay to borrow reserves from the Fed. If the economy and/or inflation is growing too rapidly, the Fed can withdraw money from the banking system, raise banking reserve requirements, or raise the discount rate, all of which slow economic growth.

▶ **M1/Money Supply:** The total amount of money in the economy, including currency in circulation, and deposits in savings and checking accounts. Most of the nation's money is in bank demand deposits, which are governed by the Federal Reserve Board. The Fed manages the nation's money supply by increasing or decreasing the reserve requirements of member banks or the discount rate at which they can borrow funds from the Fed. If there is too much money compared to the production of goods, interest rates tend to go up, and prices and output go down, causing unemployment and idle plant capacity.

▶ **Prime Rate:** The key interest rate in the U.S. economy, which is the rate charged creditworthy customers by U.S. banks. Prime rate often is determined by a bank's cost of funds and by the rates that borrowers will accept. Most small business and some consumer loans are pegged two or three points over a bank's prime rate.

▶ **Program Trading:** The computerized purchase of securities in the stock market by institutional managers who often initiate a massive buy program of all stocks in a given program or index on which options and/or futures are traded. Program trading has come under severe censure by many Wall Street experts for its contributing role in the stock market crash of October 1987.

▶ **Recessionary:** The tendency toward a downturn in economic activity, which is officially defined as at least two consecutive quarters of decline in the nation's gross national product.

▶ **Trade Deficit/Surplus:** An overage of imports relative to exports (a trade surplus is the opposite) which results in a negative balance of trade. Trading is considered all transactions in merchandise and other movable goods, as only one element of the larger current account, which includes services and tourism, transportation, interest and profits earned overseas, among other invisible items.

SMALL BUSINESSES CAN ADAPT EXISTING FUND-RAISING STRATEGIES

As the U.S. economy acknowledges and yields to the increasing globalization of domestic trade, the financial strategies that support small business and big business growth are changing, too. One of the key fund-raising strategies to undergo an abrupt change in the unique economic environment of the middle and late 1980s is the "bigger is better" strategy. As America struggles with record budget and balance of trade deficits, pending inflation, cut-throat competition from Asia, and a record-high bankruptcy rate, investors are closing their checkbooks to the initial public offering market, converting their portfolios to cash, and combing the market for value as never before. The stock market crash in October 1987 had a chilling effect on many of the individual investors who once gambled in the new issues (initial public offering) market. It took nearly one year for some of the larger institutional investors to buy back into the start-up market.

As a result, the effect on financings of nearly every size has been profound: They are smaller, they are more time-consuming to structure and sell, they are more costly, and they are based more on present value than on blue-sky projections. To get capital in the public market, a company must have significant growth potential—often similar to the capacity for growth preferred by venture capitalists. Cautious investors demand and get strength, cash flow, and experienced management in the new issues market; staying power, assets, and track record in the private equity market; and three-way protection from primary collateral, secondary collateral, and cash flow in the debt market. Now lenders want, and get, equity participations in the form of warrants for stock; equity investors are buying convertible securities from even the smallest issuers. In 1987, deep-pocketed foreign investors purchased a record number of U.S. companies, U.S. patents, and U.S. technology. In fact, many small business owners realized they could raise more money more easily in offshore markets than in the U.S. capital markets.

The financial strategy shift to "smaller is better" looks, at first, like it benefits small business owners. But "smaller" is relative, based on a universe that includes multibillion-dollar, multinational corporations. With the emerging emphasis on present value as well as on growth potential; on fundamentals like assets, sales, and earnings; on proprietary products; and on a global lockout on the competition, many entrepreneurs will find it increasingly difficult to raise $100,000 or less in start-up financing.

The most successful financings in terms of time/money saved and dollars raised are completed by business owners who do their homework before the financing as well as put the proceeds to profitable use after they locate money.

KEY YOUR OPERATION TO INDUSTRY STANDARDS

One way to leap ahead of competitors in the race for capital is to position your financial request and your presentation of the company's operations within the standards set by competitors for your industry. Unless they are experts in your industry, investors who put money into small, private companies like yours have no way of knowing whether or not your costs, sales, or earnings are high or low unless they can compare them to a competitor's performance. If you take the time to compare your numbers with industry standards, you may discover that they compare favorably—a clear signal that justifies a request for more money.

FOLLOW INFLATIONARY AND RECESSIONARY TRENDS

Only a few macroeconomic events—an increase in interest rates or a glut of foreign competitors clogging the local marketplace—influence small business in a direct way. Although most financial headlines in the nation's press can be virtually ignored by this sector, the impact of an increase in interest rates and foreign competition (by industry) should be factored into any financing request. An owner who plans ahead to solicit equity capital during an inflationary rise in rates is more likely to get maximum value for his dollar than the owner whose company's shares have been diluted by too many shareholders. The reverse is true for debt financings; when interest rates, for example, are falling, the company should be prepared to handle additional debt service in order to take advantage of the lower rates.

LOOK BEYOND LOCAL EQUITY AND DEBT SOURCES

If the global marketplace has grown exponentially during the 1980s, so has the number of financing sources now available to entrepreneurs all over the world. The business owner who isn't afraid to make inquiries about investing and lending practices in offshore markets is an owner who will be financed more often, who will access lucrative markets faster than the competition, and who will increase sales and earnings with the knowledgeable assistance of worldwide traders.

One of the surprises to a small business owner who gets financing in Europe or Asia is that the capital was not only available at

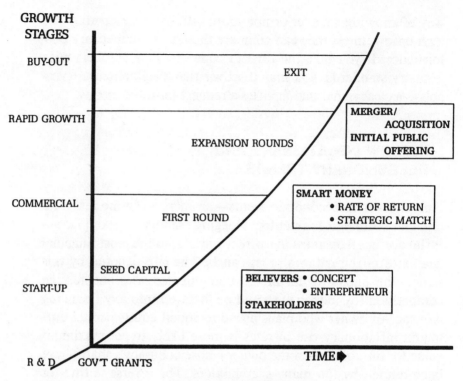

Financing for Business

Source: Ernst & Whinney

the right time, but also advanced under beneficial terms and by cooperative, long-term traders. In fact, hundreds of Americans finally received financing when they stopped pounding the pavement at home and started to look around at the global marketplace. But to attract financing, especially from overseas sources, it is important to understand how your potential investors/lenders view their investment in you.

Manufacturing Industries and Services Industries

One of the most difficult barriers in the national perception of the economy that must be overcome by small business owners is the relative position and importance of the service sector as a component of the Gross National Product. At first glance, it is difficult to understand why the companies in service industries can't get financing. Although the United States has had a service-oriented economy for over 40 years (agriculture, construction, mining, and manufacturing as the goods-producing sector has provided the minority amount of GNP employment and output), growth in the service sector has been phenomenal and continues to rise. More than 72 percent of all American workers are employed in service-sector companies. In contrast, agricultural employment is a low 3 percent and goods-producing jobs total only about 25 percent of all U.S. employment.

Part of the service-sector myth is that jobs in these industries are stultifying, low-pay opportunities. The reality is that 50 percent of all U.S. workers are in highly skilled white collar jobs. Recently, the growth rate for fast-food franchises and eating and drinking establishments has nearly doubled. Almost two-thirds of the GNP is generated by service industries; the U.S. exports about $70 billion of services annually, which is a minimum estimate, and has a 20 percent share of the $350 billion world services market.

The Bureau of Labor Statistics recently examined America's perceptions of the service sector compared to its track record and found that productivity growth was not materially different from that in the goods-producing sector. There was high capital intensity in many services and "a very negligible effect on the productivity slowdown" resulted from the recent emphasis on services. What has become more apparent in recent studies of this phenomenon is that the health of the other two sectors—manufacturing/goods-producing and technology—is closely related to the health of the service sector.

No longer can the economy function efficiently by supporting only one or two sectors at the expense of the third. Our national misconception about the service sector must be transformed into a realistic view of all three sectors operating as an industrial mix.

The lack of understanding about the role of service companies in the industrial mix is most evident when new or growing firms try to obtain financing. Lenders and debt investors avoid financing service start-ups because they lack "tangible" output, as measured in the goods-producing industries. Their collateral, measured in brains, talent, and creativity, isn't considered bankable. Standards of performance, according to investors, are too difficult to apply and production cannot be regulated. Equity investors, on the other hand, want at least the potential for speedy growth. Service companies are so labor-intensive, they say, that returns on investment take years longer to realize.

In general, service company financing now occurs at two important junctures in the company's maturity cycle. In the start-up phase, a small amount of debt financing can be raised for working capital. Most entrepreneurs who start up a service company are dismayed to find that the only capital they can raise is a limited amount of personal credit financing. In exchange for an adjustable line of credit based on personal net worth and income, the founder of a service company has to put a second mortgage on his or her residence and commit nearly all discretionary cash to the venture. A bank loan may be granted under special circumstances or as a condition of qualification for a special bank or government financing program.

The following chart illustrates one thought process that service company management can use to "prove" and support intangible measurement factors in the marketing strategy.

Basic Elements of a Strategic Service Vision

Target Market Segments:

What are common characteristics of key market segments?

What dimensions can be used to segment the market? Demographic? Psychographic?

How important are various segments?

What needs does each have?

How well are these needs being served?

Service Concept:

What are important elements of the service to be provided in results produced for customers?

How are these elements supposed to be perceived by the target market segment? By the market in general? By employees? By others?

How is the service concept perceived?

What efforts does this suggest in terms of the manner in which the

Target Market Segments:	Service Concept:
	service is designed? Delivered? Marketed?

Operating Strategy:

What are important elements of the strategy? Operations? Financing? Marketing? Organization? Human resources? Control?

On which will the most effort be concentrated?

Where will investments be made?

How will quality and cost be controlled? Measures? Incentives? Rewards?

What results will be expected vs. competition in terms of quality of service? Cost profile? Productivity? Morale/loyalty of servers?

Service Delivery System:

What are important elements of the service delivery system? Role of people? Technology? Equipment? Facilities? Layout? Procedures?

What capacity does it provide? Normally? At peak levels?

To what extent does it help insure quality standards? Differentiate the service from competition? Provide barriers to entry by competition?

Source: James L. Heskett, "Managing in the Service Economy," Harvard Business School.

When the company is on solid financial footing and can justify an expansion of operations, a small amount of equity capital can be raised to fund the expansion. This equity financing may come from a private placement or exempt offering to sophisticated investors who understand the company's industry or from corporate partners in the form of a joint venture, marketing agreement, or licensing agreement, among other forms.

In the pages that follow, we address the special financing needs of service companies, a sector that tends to be ignored or underrated by both debt and equity investors. The viability of each fund-raising strategy for both manufacturing and service companies is indicated and described in Chapter 1.

One desirable trait for an entrepreneur is the ability to disclose proprietary information about the company appropriately and adequately. If you are raising an initial round of financing, review the questions below as an indication of what equity investors and lenders want to know about your business.

*The Entrepreneurial Personality:**

- Do you like to make your own decisions?

- Do you enjoy competition?

- Do you have willpower and self-discipline?

- Do you plan ahead?

- Do you get things done on time?

- Can you take advice from others?

- Are you adaptable to changing conditions?

- Do you know that owning your own business may entail working up to 16 hours a day, probably six days a week, and maybe on holidays?

- Do you have the physical stamina to handle a business?

- Do you have the emotional strength to withstand the strain?

- Are you prepared to lower your standard of living for several months or years?

- Are you prepared to lose your savings?

Personal Considerations:

- Do you know which skills and areas of expertise are critical to your success?

- Do you have these skills?

- Does your idea effectively utilize your own skills and abilities?

- Can you find personnel that have the expertise you lack?

- Do you know why you are considering this business?

- Will your project effectively meet your career aspirations?

**Source:* U.S. Small Business Administration

Project Description:

- Briefly describe the business you want.

- List the products and/or services you will sell.

- Describe who will use your product.

- Why would someone buy your product?

- What kind of location do you need, such as neighborhood, traffic count, and nearby firms?

- List your product/raw material suppliers.

- List your major competitors.

- List the labor and staff you require to provide your products.

Success Requirements:

- Does your product or business serve a need that is currently unserved?

- Does your product or business serve an existing market in which demand exceeds supply?

- Can the product or business successfully compete with existing competition because of an advantageous situation, such as better price or prime location?

Major Flaws:

- Are there any causes that make any of the required factors of production unavailable, for example, unreasonable costs, scarce skills, energy, material, equipment, processes, technology, or personnel?

- Are capital requirements for entry or continuing operations excessive?

- Is adequate financing hard to obtain?

- Are there potential detrimental environmental effects?
- Are there factors that prevent effective marketing?

Desired Income:

- How much income do you want?
- Are you prepared to earn less income in the first one to three years?
- What minimum income do you require?
- What financial investment will be required for your business?
- How much could you earn by investing this money?
- How much could you earn by working for someone else?
- Add the amounts from the two preceding questions. If this income is greater than what you can realistically expect from your business, are you prepared to forego this additional income just to be your own boss with only the prospect of more substantial income in future years?
- What is the average return on investment for a business of your type?

Preliminary Income Statement:

- What is the normal markup in this line of business?
- What is the average cost of goods sold as a percentage of sales?
- What is the average inventory turnover annually?
- What is the average gross profit as a percentage of sales?
- What are the average expenses as a percentage of sales?
- What is the average net profit as a percentage of sales?
- Take the preceding figures and work backwards using a standard income statement format and determine the level of sales necessary to support your desired income level.

- Realistically, is this level of sales, expenses, and profit attainable?

Market Analysis: Population

- Define the geographical areas from which you can realistically expect to draw customers.
- What is the population of these areas?
- What do you know about the population growth trend in these areas?
- What is the average family size, age distribution, per capita income?
- What are the consumers' attitudes toward businesses like yours?
- What do you know about consumer shopping and spending patterns relative in your business?
- Is the price of your product/service important to your target market?
- Can you appeal to the entire market?
- If you can appeal to only a market segment, is it large enough to be profitable?

Competition:

- Who are your major competitors?
- What are the major strengths of each?
- What are the major weaknesses of each?
- Do you know your competitors' pricing structure, product lines, location, promotional activities, supply sources, and image among consumers?
- Do you know of any new competitors?
- Do you know of any competitor's plans for expansion?

- Have any firms like yours gone out of business lately?

- Do you know the sales and market share of each competitor?

- Do you know whether the sales and market share of each competitor are increasing, decreasing, or stable?

- Do you know the profit levels of each competitor?

- Are your competitors' profits increasing, decreasing, or stable?

- Can you compete with your competition?

Sales:

- Determine the total sales volume in your market area.

- How accurate do you think your forecast of total sales is?

- Did you base your forecast on concrete data?

- Is the estimated sales figure "normal" for your market area?

- Is the sales per square foot for your competitors above the normal average?

- Are there conditions, or trends, that could change your forecast of total sales?

- Do you expect to carry items in inventory seasonally, or do you plan to mark down products occasionally to eliminate inventories?

- How do you plan to advertise and promote your product or business?

- Forecast the share of the total market that you can realistically expect as a dollar amount and as a percentage of your market.

- Are you sure that you can create enough competitive advantages to achieve the market share in your forecast of the previous question?

- Is your forecast of dollar sales greater than the sales amount needed to guarantee your desired or minimum income?

- Have you been optimistic or pessimistic in your forecast of sales?

- Do you need to hire an expert to refine the sales forecast?

- Are you willing to hire an expert to refine the sales forecast?

Supply:

- Can you make a list of every item of inventory and operating supplies needed?

- Do you know the quantity, quality, technical specifications, and price ranges desired?

- Do you know the name and location of each potential source of supply?

- Do you know the price ranges available for each product from each supplier?

- Do you know delivery schedules for each supplier?

- Do you know the sales terms of each supplier?

- Do you know the credit terms of each supplier?

- Do you know the financial condition of each supplier?

- Is there a risk of shortage for any critical materials or merchandise?

- Are you aware of which supplies have an advantage relative to transportation costs?

- Will the price available allow you to achieve an adequate markup?

Expenses:

- Do you know what your expenses will be for rent, wages, insurance, utilities, advertising, interest?

- Do you need to know which expenses are direct, indirect, or fixed?

- Do you know how much your overhead will be?

- Do you know how much your selling expenses will be?

Miscellaneous:

- Are you aware of the major risks associated with your product? Business?

- Can you minimize any of these major risks?

- Are there major risks beyond your control?

- Can these risks bankrupt you?

CHAPTER 1

Determining How Much Capital to Raise

▸ **Commercial Paper:** Short-term issues that usually are discounted obligations with maturities of 2 to 270 days, issued by banks, corporations, and other borrowers to lenders/investors with large amounts of cash on hand. These IOUs, some of which are interest-bearing, are issued directly or indirectly through brokers by top-rated companies that are backed by a bank line of credit.

▸ **Equity:** The portion of company ownership possessed by shareholders, in contrast to debt as a junior or senior claim against repayment from the company.

▸ **Hybrid (Convertible) Security:** A security with the features of both debt and equity, usually structured as a bond or debenture that is later convertible to common stock at a preset price.

▸ **Investment Bank:** A firm that acts as underwriter or agent between a stock-issuing company and the investing public. The firm offers preunderwriting counseling, document preparation, offering sales and distribution of securities, followed by ongoing guidance and board membership after the offering is completed. An investment banker acts as an intermediary to sell a company's shares offering firm commitment, best effort, or standby commitment.

▸ **Merchant Banking:** A transaction in which an investment bank acts not only as the intermediary for clients to help raise money, but also as an investor with in-house capital riding on the invested. Merchant bankers want returns from the investment; investment bankers look for fees to arrange the deal. Traditional merchant banking is prevalent in Europe and Asia; in the United States, this function is often indistinguishable from investment banking or venture capital.

▸ **Subordinated Debt:** Debt that is junior to other debt (senior debt) in its claim on assets for repayment.

▸ **Valuation:** The estimation of a private company's market value by comparison with the market value of similar public companies and with industry standards among other similar private firms; usually conducted by professional industry consultants. Corporate valuations rise and fall as interest rates rise and fall; equity financing is worth more when interest rates go up, while debt or bond financing is worth more when rates go down.

The place to start planning a corporate financing is right in your own cash register: How much money will your business yield from operations to meet future working capital or growth needs? Figure 1.1 illustrates the sources of internal financing that exist in every business.

The most effective way to raise a small amount of capital in any economic environment is to picture the fund-raising process as an equation: The amount you think you need must be balanced by the amount your company is qualified to raise. The amount of money you think you need should be a compromise between your dollar projections and the amounts raised by comparable companies in your industry—public or private.

If you place the projections within the financing range for your industry or within geographically similar markets, for example, you are signaling investors that you've grounded your numbers in reality. When small business funding is stingy because of high interest rates, stock market jitters, or any reason, investors need extra assurance that their investment in your high-risk venture will pay off. Drawing favorable comparisons between your business and previously successful fund-raisers will give them that assurance and give you higher proceeds.

To estimate the second half of the equation—the amount your company is qualified to raise from debt and equity sources—requires a realistic review of the most appropriate potential sources of $100,000 or less, and some knowledge about how they package and transact a small business investment.

THE FIRST HALF OF THE EQUATION: VALUATING YOUR COMPANY AND A COMPARABLE COMPANY

In order to sell your financial request convincingly to debt or equity investors, it is important to validate such factors as the corporate mission statement, marketing strategies, and the financial request so that your solicitation is grounded in the reality of your industry and/or market. Your projections are important, but

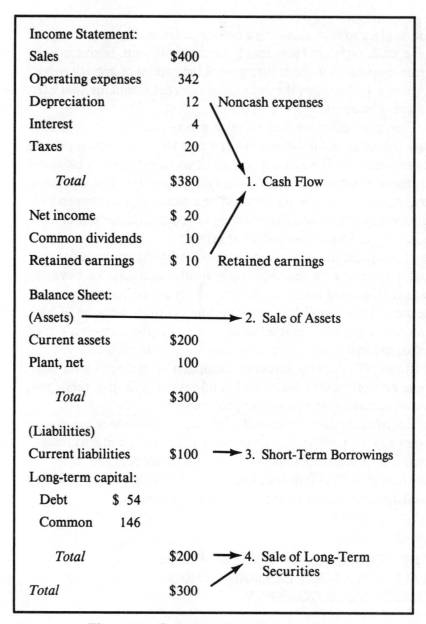

Figure 1.1 Sources of Internal Funding

they should be augmented by the results achieved when comparable companies were financed. This requires that you identify two or three comparable companies in your industry/market, valuate your business in comparison with them, and then adjust the amount you request to the level of their financings.

If you have no idea where to start, start with the government's Standard Industrial Classification (SIC) Code system. Your number will identify the industry you serve, and the industry subgroup; the same is true for any competitor's SIC number. A four-digit number is assigned to identify a business based on the type of business or trade involved. The first two digits correspond to major groups, such as construction and manufacturing. The last two numbers correspond to subgroups, such as constructing homes or constructing highways. You can determine your SIC number by looking it up in a directory published by the Department of Commerce, or by checking the SIC book in the reference section of a local library. The SBA's company size standards, for example, are based on SIC codes.

The easiest way to valuate and compare your business, of course, is to acquire the annual/quarterly reports and related documentation of a similar public company that has complied with Securities & Exchange Commission requirements to disclose the financial and other information you need to complete your valuation comparison. Private companies are not required to disclose this information, so it can be difficult to acquire the appropriate financial information that is needed to valuate and compare a private firm. At minimum, try to compare at least these basic criteria:

- Same or peripheral industries
- Financial characteristics
- Minimum size
- Market niche
- Profitability

The establishing criteria for same or related industries should include:

- Growth prospects
- Cyclicality
- Competitive environment
- Ease of entry
- Labor/capital intensity
- Regulatory effects

The establishing criteria for profitability should include:

- Risk/stability
- Quality
- Payback
- Growth rate
- Return on investment (ROI)
- Capital expenditures

The amount of due diligence required to investigate the factors listed above will yield only basic information about a private company. It is enough data to make a rough comparison, but not enough to apply professional valuation methods. With more due diligence from some of the sources listed below, it is possible to activate a professional valuation method used by investment bankers, merger/acquisition specialists, and CPAs.

U.S. Census Data

This source is a gold mine for information about specific industries as a whole and the products sold within their market parameters. You will find dollar volume costs, product specifications, total retail sales, and sales projections, which are helpful in calculating the relative value of the sales and the marketing campaign of the company under scrutiny.

Syndicated Service Data

Most companies use research and reporting services that store data in certain product categories and industries, including market share, total sales, sales behavior and consumer choices, brand loyalty and attrition, and purchase and nonpurchase biases. These firms use detailed diaries that are filled out by households and industry buyers, electronic ratings services for radio and television viewership, magazine readership definition, product placement records, individual store audits, and consumer interviews.

Previous Litigation

Almost all documents related to litigation are a matter of public record as trial proceedings. The transcripts of evidence introduced in trials and in pretrial depositions, therefore, become a rich source of information about your competitors, including complaint and answer documents, adversaries' briefs, and court decisions. From this paperwork, you will pick up a lot of information about the structure and substance of the industry, the company, and the marketing problems inherent in the sales environment.

Trade Publications

There is a vast amount of revealing information about many companies in the trade press, which often covers such aspects of operations as company policies, personalities, sales, and special problems. Often, these media will publish in-depth speeches made by current and past corporate officers. It is helpful to hire a clipping service to search on a regular basis for information that has been printed about two or three comparable companies.

Marketing Analysis

If you can afford the service, commission a marketing analysis by a professional firm that has specialized in your industry and knows the facts behind the numbers. The essential discovery you want is a situation analysis of the major competitors in the industry and their relative ranking in total sales volume (market share), production level, marketing policies, profit as a percent of total sales or as a return on investment, diversity of products, and relative profits. Also have the firm look at the trends generated by this data over the past five-year and 24-month periods, and the projections for the next 24-month and five-year periods.

Compiling Industry Standards

From these sources, you can begin to compile the industry standards with which your costs will be compared. Table 1.1 illustrates a helpful comparison model.

After you have collected data on two or three similar companies, you can begin to compare their operations to your company

Table 1.1
Costs of Doing Business for Proprietorships

Industry	Selected Costs (as Percent)				
	Cost/ Gds	Purchases	Labor	Supplies	Gross Margin
Retail	72.4	66.7	1.3	1.1	27.6
Wholesale	74.8	66.8	0.7	0.9	25.2
Manufacturing	40.1	24.3	17.7	6.1	59.9
Construction	47.3	17.7	8.3	13.5	52.7
Service	18.7	10.6	2.8	2.4	81.4
Transportation/ Utilities	19.2	11.2	2.5	1.0	80.8
Finance/ Insurance/RE	19.7	6.2	0.5	0.3	80.4
Mining	19.9	10.4	1.1	0.6	80.1
Agric./Forestry/ Fishing	17.4	26.8	4.4	3.6	62.6

Source: "Statistics of Income," Sole Proprietorships Income Tax Returns, U.S. Treasury, Internal Revenue Service, Individual Returns Analysis Section

by applying a valuation method. There are seven ways to compare your business to a competitor or a similar, noncompetitive company in another market:

- *By Replacement Value:* The amount of capital required to replace or reproduce the business in its entirety by acquiring replacement assets in the marketplace at fair market value.

- *By Present Value of Cash Flow:* The value of the company's cash flow adjusted for the time value of money and the business/economic risks.

- *By Liquidation Value:* The valuation of nonoperating assets only. Operating assets and income produced by such assets are valued separately.

- *By Book Value:* (Also net tangible asset or adjusted book value) Book value is total assets minus total liabilities, with adjustments for intangibles like goodwill. Adjusted book value is based on adjustments for equipment or place depreciation, land/real estate appreciation, or inventory fluctuations resulting from the accounting method.

- *By Formula (or Factor):* A valuation based on combined earnings, dividend-capability, and book value.

- *By Earnings:* This is an investor's favorite method for calculating return on investment (ROI). First, true earnings are reviewed, with adjustments for operating years and other factors. Then a multiple generally is applied: it is higher for a low-risk business, lower for a high-risk venture.

- *By Combinations of the Above Values and Formulae:* When a professional valuation is made for the sale of a company, most willing corporate buyers and sellers, the Internal Revenue Service, and the court system prefer that a combination of valuation methods be used in order to get the broadest base of information. But it is important to know that there is no one correct method or combination of methods.

The idea is to use whatever method is appropriate and makes the comparison easy to perform. The most frequent combination is earnings—a multiple of earnings—and liquidation values. In most manufacturing and service industries, the question underlying the creation of any fund-raising strategy is whether cash flow or earnings will be valued more by investors when they evaluate a financing request. On the basis of that determination and others, a strategy is conceived from corporate financial strength rather than from weakness. The golden mean, of course, is to look at cash-flow potential but check to see that its effect on earnings isn't unnecessarily negative.

If your comparable company is in the oil and gas industry, for example, and wants to become a buyout candidate, the energy firm most likely will use a present value approach to cash flow. This method values the estimated stream of cash that the company can produce, indicating the value of the company as a whole. When cash flows are discounted, the discount rate provides a comparison of the investment in the firm to other buyout opportunities for the investors. Incidentally, present value also indicates the maximum price an investor should pay for the oil and gas company.

For private companies in manufacturing industries, a simple cash-flow model is easy to apply—although there are highly complex, highly interactive models available for the public company. The cash-flow analyzed is net cash generated by operations, excluding financing costs. If you don't have much information about a competitor in this category, you can use Operating Cash Flow:

	Net income (adjusted)
plus:	Depreciation
less:	Planned capital expenditures
less:	Changes in working capital
equals:	Operating cash flow

The "Bottom Up" cash-flow model is used by more dynamic or larger manufacturing companies to estimate sales and direct expenses product line by product line. Advertising and R&D budgets are reviewed, and forecasts are made for several years into the future.

Depending on how good a financial detective you are in

acquiring at least some information about comparable companies, begin the comparison process by analyzing several sets of ratios that indicate key facts about their operations. They include liquidity ratios, which measure how well the company meets current obligations; leverage ratios, which measure the amount of debt-financed operations and expenditures; activity ratios, which measure how efficiently the company utilizes assets; and profitability ratios, which measure returns from sales and investments. A comparison of many other ratios would fine-tune your analysis even further; but an in-depth financial comparison isn't necessary for the amount of capital you are trying to raise. If the comparable company you have selected is a public entity, the market value of its stock must be handicapped to the value of your privately held corporation so that you can show investors an apples-to-apples comparison:

- Calculate earnings per share (EPS) for three to five years.
- Determine average price per share (APS).
- Calculate the price-earnings (P/E) ratio by dividing APS by EPS.
- Calculate the average price/earnings ratio.
- Apply the average P/E ratio to average EPS for five years.

There are drawbacks to using the comparable method of valuating a small, privately held business in a solicitation of private investors, but none of them is a deal-killer if you address the issues early on. To avoid unfavorable comparisons from potential investors, make sure your comparable companies are roughly the same size, use the same accounting method, compare in depth of management, and produce the same number of products.

THE SECOND HALF OF THE EQUATION: WHO INVESTS $100,000 OR LESS IN SMALL BUSINESS VENTURES

One of the key rules of capitalizing a company is: There are no right and wrong funding amounts—no matter how high or how low—but there are wrong sources from which to expect funding as low as $100,000 or less. You are more likely to get the financing you need if you approach appropriate capital sources with a request that reflects their investment specifications. This means you wouldn't try to open a retail clothing shop with $100,000 in debt funding from a venture capitalist. You would know before you make the financial request that venture capital firms look for minimum investments of $500,000 to $1 million, that they prefer high-tech products to any retail business, and that they are equity, not debt, investors.

In the same way, a cursory review of the market for initial public offerings would reveal that a retail store wouldn't be an IPO candidate: successful IPOs have assets and cash flow, significant growth potential, proprietary products, and depth of management, among other characteristics that are unusual for a small business. Following is a review of the equity and debt capital sources that can be accessed by a small business owner who has tailored his or her funding request to the strategy preferred by the source.

Financing Techniques to Access Equity Capital Sources

Friends and Family (F&F)

This capital pool can surprise you: Friends and family can be good for everything from $100 to cover your monthly telephone bill when you really need it up to $100,000 for sophisticated, first-round financing that serves as working capital for one full year of operation. Most entrepreneurs approach friends and family cautiously, selling small units of ownership or debt in the $1,000 to $5,000 range. The trick is to get enough capital the first time, but not ask for too much, so you won't have to go back to the same well too often. The best way to approach friends and family on a continuing basis, through two or three rounds of small financings, is to make good on your promise of first-round returns or loan payments before making the second solicitation.

The Benefit: F&F is the cheapest form of equity, it doesn't take much time to raise, and these investors often are more forgiving of nonperformance than public or other private investors. They are definitely more forgiving than lenders.

The Risk: Unless you get everything in writing, F&F disputes can be more difficult and take more time to resolve than outside-investor disputes. Before you ask friends and family to invest, decide how much and what level of participation in the business is acceptable to you.

Service/Manufacturing Companies: F&F financing is a good vehicle for service-oriented companies that are too small or too new to have what early-stage lenders are looking for: collateral in the form of salable assets, cash or revenue flow, or a track record on which to base projections. Use F&F capital to establish a customer base and a revenue base. Then apply for second-stage financing in the form of a loan. Capital-intensive manufacturing and technology companies generally need more cash than is available from F&F sources unless you are looking for a short-term fix.

Exempt Offerings

The IPO market bonanza in the early 1980s financed small companies at fantastic pricing levels for several years. But when it crashed, up and coming IPO hopefuls looked to the private equity market to balance the scarcity of public funding. Exempt offerings replaced IPOs as the funding vehicle of choice. Entrepreneurs who sold exempt offerings assumed correctly that equity dollars were available to them in small amounts from private sources; but without a supportive IPO market, small, closely held companies now had to pay more for private funding. It is still a problem, because the cheapest form of debt is not accessible to seed companies, and venture capitalists are using available capital to shore up portfolio companies in which they already have a sizable investment.

Not surprisingly, equity investors are more risk-averse than they used to be. They are asking entrepreneurs to accept more of the risk by accepting more conservative valuations. The discounting trend since the market crash in 1987 is contingent on your company's development stage and industry: start-ups, which are valued more on earnings potential, have suffered less markdown than later-stage companies, which are valued by comparison with similar public companies.

Industries with the highest P/E ratios before the crash, that is, high technology and biotechnology, have been marked down up to 60 percent in contrast to markdowns of only 20 percent on manufacturing and service companies with lower P/E ratios for the same period.

Although institutional and retail investors had brought the IPO market nearly to a close in October 1987, many entrepreneurs took another look at the IPO market in early 1988 and decided it was slightly more receptive than the year before. With the growth of new IPO activity, private investors loosened their pursestrings once again.

The easiest stock offering for a financing of $100,000 or less is still the 504 exempt offering. Typically, it generates from $100,000 to $500,000 (maximum) in equity capital, but it can be whittled down even further to raise as little as $50,000 or $75,000 if that is all you need. Keep in mind that private equity investors have continued to use more stringent investment criteria than they did before the October 1987 stock market crash, including earnings potential, depth of management, and assets with which to weather economic volatility.

Many of the other exempt offerings are almost always inappropriate for raising small amounts of cash from private investors:

Full Registration:

Form S-1:   No dollar limit

Exempt or Limited Offerings:

504 Exempt offering: Up to $500,000

505 Exempt offering: Up to $5 million

506 Exempt offering: No dollar limit

Private placement: Up to $5 million

(Section 4(6)):

147 Offering:	No dollar limit

Simplified Registration:

Form S-18:	Up to $7.5 million
Reg A offering:	Up to $1.5 million

Limited partnerships are another way to access the private equity market. Private offerings of this tax-driven issue can be sold to a maximum of 35 nonaccredited investors and an unlimited number of accredited investors, each of whom contributes $25,000 to $50,000 per unit, or more to the total investment.

The Benefit: Private equity sources remain willing to finance deals that the IPO market has rejected as too small. There is minimal reporting/disclosure compliance required by the SEC and state regulators in contrast to the offering requirements of the public market.

The Risk: Private equity is now nearly as expensive as public equity because of the decline in initial public offering activity since the mid-1980s. Unless your company has cash flow, salable assets, and a strong and deep management team, private investors will scrutinize your deal more closely than ever to weed out high-risk ventures. They may ask you to assume some of the risk yourself.

Service/Manufacturing Companies: An exempt offering to the private market is one of the best ways to finance a service business. These investors often are specialists in certain industries; if they like your industry and your company, they can become "True Believers" whose pockets deepen as your need for increased capital grows.

Resource Possibility: A.G. Edwards & Sons/St. Louis, MO

Joint Ventures/Technology
Transfer Agreements

Joint venture, technology transfer, research and development, and licensing agreements can be the most flexible way to generate cash in the small business sector, generating from as little as $25,000 to as much as $5 million. These agreements generally confer certain other benefits to you as the owner of a product or technology—including facilities, expertise, and/or materials resources—so the ratio of capital to benefits for the entrepreneur in the deal can vary widely.

Transfer technology agreements are of particular interest to offshore corporations and government agencies that want to buy rights to manufacture, market, and/or distribute your product or technology back home. They will usually pay a premium over U.S. companies if your product/technology is unavailable in their local market, if your technology can enhance their technical infrastructure, or if they can develop future products by owning yours.

The Benefit: These agreements allow you to profit from developing or inventing a new product without the increased responsibility of managing a growing company; it gives you a cash stake with which to start a new company or retire. Tech transfer agreements, in particular, attract offshore investors who may become long-term trading partners, allowing you to penetrate foreign markets more easily and profitably.

The Risk: You may sign away more ownership rights to your product or technology than you intend unless you have competent outside advice from professionals who specialize in offshore agreements and in your industry. Your product or technology should be well defined and patent-protected, if applicable, for both domestic and offshore markets so you do not lose product spin-offs, or special terms and rights. Performance benchmarks for the licensee should be written into every contract to avoid loss of sales and earnings from an inactive licensee.

Service/Manufacturing Companies: Service companies generally don't attract joint venture or technology transfer partners unless the service is highly specialized, in demand in the marketplace, or is complementary to the manufacturing/technology mix of the agreement partner. Most of these agreements are structured specifically to commercialize a manufactured product or a technology.

Resource Possibilities: Dean Witter Reynolds, Inc./Washington, DC

tku Technologies, Ltd./Englewood, CO

Consulate General/People's Republic of China/Chicago, IL

Merchant Banking

Some investment banks in the United States provide a merchant banking function, in which the brokerage house invests its own cash to sell out a client offering. Merchant banking in the United States applies most often to large deals of over $1 million, which can be difficult to sell when certain economic indicators are present. The amount of the investment is usually equal to the value of the shares that remain unsold. Offshore merchant banks frequently finance small U.S. companies with a combination of debt and equity capital, starting at the $100,000 to $200,000 level.

The Benefit: Offshore merchant banks that function as a financing arm of their governments can compete aggressively for your business with highly lucrative tax breaks; incentive allowances in the form of cash, land, buildings, and equipment; and long-term trading opportunities in foreign markets that are difficult to access from the United States. Here, investment banks that put their own money into your deal can make it a more successful offering financially than brokerage houses that act merely as underwriters or that fail to sell out the offering.

The Risk: The long-term requirements demanded by offshore merchant banks increase the cost of financing your company in the future, including such expensive issues as the environmental impact of your company and the need to create new jobs in the offshore market.

Service/Manufacturing Companies: Most merchant banks in the United States prefer investing in manufacturing and technology companies, although highly specialized services have been financed by this source. Offshore merchant banks, which often are more debt-oriented than their counterparts in the United States, always prefer to lend against the collateral and cash flow generated by manufacturing and technology companies.

Resource Possibilities: IDA Ireland, Industrial Development Authority/San Francisco, CA

United Bank of Denver, Merchant Banking Group/Denver, CO

Public Offerings

Most initial public offerings of stock in start-up companies are priced at the $1 million level, which is usually the smallest offering sold by a local underwriter. Regional underwriters like IPO deals that start at $5 million; national underwriters sell the largest IPOs, starting at about $25 million.

Going public overseas usually doesn't make sense unless you want to raise $500,000 or more, although some companies have raised as little as $100,000 to $150,000 on the London and Tokyo stock exchanges, primarily due to poor sales. If you take your company public on an offshore exchange, you probably won't raise more money from investors than you would in the United States, but you may decrease certain filing and third-party expenses significantly. Until the mid-1980s, it cost about 50 percent less to go public overseas; recent changes in the regulations governing such international markets as The Stock Exchange in London have evened out the costs.

Public limited partnerships, including research and development, income, and other specialized partnership offerings start at about $200,000, although there have been a few smaller limited partnership offerings, and they raise up to $20 million for large corporations.

Warrants for stock are another market vehicle for raising small amounts of equity capital. The key to warrant pricing, and the amount of your equity infusion, is the balance among maturity date, the nature of your company, and special warrant terms. To estimate the amount of equity it's possible to raise, select one of the common pricing strategies:

1. Price the warrants the same as the common; or

2. Estimate the market price of the common at a future date and from that date, calculate the current price based on an annual percent return that investors are likely to accept.

The Benefit: Your company will have a broader equity base as a public entity, and a larger net asset value. The resulting improvement in your debt/equity ratio makes it as easy, at least theoretically, to raise future equity financing as to borrow additional capital.

Service/Manufacturing Companies: Since the stock market crash of October 1987, most IPO underwriters have raised their qualifications for new issues to include higher earnings, more management depth and the creation/growth of assets. This means manufacturing/technology firms, with definable products and higher growth potential, tend to receive more attention from the new-issues market than service companies.

Resource Possibilities: E.F. Hutton & Company, Inc./New York, NY

Piper, Jaffray & Hopwood/Minneapolis, MN

Employee Stock Option Plans

The Employee Stock Option Plan (ESOP) is a stock bonus trust that can borrow funds on behalf of your employees in order to raise money to buy shares in your company for substantial or 100 percent ownership. Because ESOPs are funded with capital from your employees, this vehicle can generate up to $100,000 or more in capital for the company depending on the size of your staff. The company issues stock to an employee trust that is vested like a pension plan. When your employees leave the company, they get their vested shares or sell them back to the trust. This means the corporation gets tax benefits, often to the point of being virtually tax-exempt; individual employees get other tax deductions.

An ESOP is a tax-driven benefit plan that functions like a credit mechanism. The vested interests of its employee-investor base makes this financing strategy easier to sell than non-ESOP offerings to the public market. If your company is publicly owned, it can be taken private with an ESOP over a period of years.

There are more than 9 thousand ESOPs in the United States, covering more than 9 million employee-owners. The percent of ESOP firms in the manufacturing sector decreased from 42 to 33 percent, while service sector companies rose 3 percent.

The Benefits: They are numerous. Studies show that ESOP companies are more productive because employees are more vested in corporate interests, tend to operate free of litigation when the founder retires because of new exit opportunities, improve employee estate planning, and prevent hostile, outside takeovers.

The Risk: Stock holding opportunities must be distributed fairly among management and staff levels to avoid potential legal problems, the stock market impacts the price of employee stock, and certain financing options are foreclosed when the company is publicly held.

Service/Manufacturing Companies: Service/technology firms fare well as ESOPs because of intense employee loyalty that results in a strong aftermarket for the stock. In 1988, only about one-third of all ESOP companies were manufacturing concerns.

Resource Possibilities: Quist Financial, Inc./Boulder, CO

Employee Stock Option Association/Washington, DC

Corporate Partnering

Small companies can raise $100,000 to $1 million+ and get the free use of resources and management/technical expertise—from a large corporate partner through the use of a licensing, technology transfer, research & development, marketing/manufacturing, or joint venture agreement. Most corporate agreements cluster at the low end of the capital-raising range, depending on the extent of the other resources available to you per the contract. (This is in addition to management and other fees negotiated for special services you provide the company.)

When the licensee or partner is an offshore corporation that wants ownership of your product or technology, expect to raise 10 to 20 percent more from the deal than you would get from a U.S. partner.

The Benefits: Larger partners can provide whatever your company lacks in resources, capital, expertise, sales, or distribution at a lower-than-market cost to you; new domestic and global markets can be penetrated more quickly and with less capital when you have a partner; you can compete against rival firms more effectively with your partner's resources; your time is available to develop and extend the product/technology line; and you can strengthen your company over time to function with or without the partner.

The Risk: You may lose more ownership rights to your product/technology than you need to without leverage in the partnership; your corporate partner may prefer only a short-term project that under-compensates you; or the company's growth is weakened over the long-term.

Service/Manufacturing Companies: Corporate partnering, similar to joint venture and technology transfer agreements, tends to work well for manufacturing and technology companies that have a specific and complementary product or process to commercialize. Service companies can use partnering when the service is highly specialized, fits the specific need of a larger firm, or is in demand in the marketplace.

Resource Possibilities: Coopers & Lybrand/National Emerging Business Services/Indianapolis, IN

Embassy of the People's Republic of China/Washington, DC

Mergers/Buyouts

The amount of money you can raise from a merger, buyout or sale is dependent on the pricing multiple used in your industry, in most cases. The multiple, which can be widely variable, is generally applied to your company's earnings, book value, or market value based on a similar public company: The pricing formula would read "ten times earnings" or "ten times book value." (This capital is in addition to earnout cash paid to the owner for consulting services during the transition, stock in the acquiring company, and/or other kickers offered by the buyer.) The most appealing private-company buyouts are firms in which the principal owners hold 20 to 40 percent of the stock, the rest of the stock is widely held, the owners are in key management positions, and enough liquidity in the stock exists so that a realistic market price can be established.

If the acquiring company or senior partner is a foreign corporation or government agency, it's possible to raise 10 to 20 percent more cash, on average, from the transaction if your product or technology is not available in the buyer's country.

The Benefit: Existing companies and products usually are cheaper to acquire than start-up companies and products are to build from the ground up. A merger or buyout can be an excellent exit strategy for founders who want cash upfront, plus an earnout transition period over time in the form of salary compensation and/or royalties for profit performance.

The Risk: Start-up costs can decline, making a merger or acquisition more expensive as a percent of replacement costs; you may negotiate a one-time-only cash settlement that is too low in terms of industry growth, the value of your cutting-edge product or technology, or market conditions.

Service/Manufacturing Companies: Mergers and buyouts are an excellent strategy for small service companies that want the protection and access to corporate resources that larger companies can provide. Service companies also can use them as a safe harbor when the cost of debt goes up or when economic conditions are volatile.

Resource Possibilities: DQ Investments, Inc./AIBC Investment Services, Inc./Miami, FL

Venture Capital

If you're looking for $100,000 or less, you're probably not a candidate for pure venture capital in the eyes of U.S. or overseas investors. The smallest deals, structured by firms that manage a seed fund to specialize in high-risk start-ups in the earliest stages of development, usually start in the $500,000 to $1 million range. A few venture capital seed funds associated with private or public incubators invest at the $100,000 level. Traditional venture firms don't consider financing a company if it needs less than $1 million or $2 million, in the United States or overseas. Later-stage funds often provide $5 million or more to larger companies in a last round of financing before the companies go public or exit through a sale or merger. Occasionally, a foreign venture capital firm or a foreign merchant bank with a venture capital component will invest $200,000 or $300,000 in a small U.S. company that looks like a superstar: It has a proprietary product in a cutting-edge industry, unlimited growth potential, no competitors to date, management depth and credentials, a high earnings curve, and that indefinable quality that says it's a winner.

The Benefit: Venture capital encourages the fastest corporate growth pattern, with built-in returns and exit options for all parties to the financing. Another benefit is that portfolio companies receive a lot of free, hands-on management assistance when the company needs it most. The returns from a successful venture financing are nearly always exponentially higher than the returns earned on other forms of financing like corporate partnering or private stock offerings.

The Risk: Many venture capital firms negotiate control of the company upfront, or take over control when you and your management team are unable to attain benchmark performance standards. Even when the venture firm doesn't have a majority of your shares, the equity give-up to venture capitalists is usually high. Also, the exit strategy preferred by your venture capitalist for maximum returns may not be in the best interests of you or the company.

Service/Manufacturing Companies: Venture capitalists almost never finance service businesses unless they are highly unusual because these firms seldom have valuable assets, are dependent for revenue on unreliable human factors, and are limited in growth potential. They like manufacturing and technology companies because they have far greater growth capacity and a definable product.

Resource Possibility: Merrill Lynch Venture Capital, Inc./New York, NY

Example: Baton Rouge Business & Technology Center/Baton Rouge, LA

Government Programs

The Small Business Investment Research (SBIR) program offers working capital to small U.S. and sometimes foreign companies that bid for the opportunity to a complete research and development project, and/or commercialize a proprietary product, for the U.S. government. Phase I provides up to $50,000 for six months of feasibility-related experimental or theoretical research on topics of significant interest to the government. This phase of the program allows only a very small profit margin, if any; but successful completion of Phase I permits you to bid for a Phase 2 contract, which provides up to $500,000 for two years of related research and development of those projects that look most promising from Phase I. Phase 3 funding, to commercialize the resulting product or technology, is raised in the private sector and is limited only by the joint effort between you and the government to generate funding.

The Benefit: The company, by winning the bid for a specified project, is recognized, by definition, as an expert in its industry. Although it takes perseverance, advancement to follow-on phases of research and development in the SBIR program, for example, bring increasing infusions of capital into the company. If you want to commercialize your product or technology outside the government market and/or in foreign markets, the agency that awarded your contract will help immeasurably with market analyses, contract negotiation, distribution, and sales services.

The Risk: Faulty compliance on your part to the vast body of disclosure and reporting requirements of the U.S. government can cause you to lose some or all of your ownership rights to the product/technology you develop in the government program. This applies during the R&D as well as the commercialization stage. The government's review of your corporation legal and financial documentation may be extensive, depending on variable factors. If the government owns the rights to your product or technology, you have no recourse if it fails to commercialize or sell it.

There are a myriad of federal government financing programs and hundreds of state programs that offer small amounts of both debt and equity capital to business owners. See Chapter 3 and the government resource lists in the Appendix for more information.

Service/Manufacturing Companies: Most government programs are debt-oriented, which means manufacturing and technology companies will have the edge on getting this financing. Equity-oriented programs like SBIR, in Phases 2 and 3, also prefer these sectors because the financing programs have been structured to commercialize specific products and technologies required by the federal government.

Resource Possibilities: Department of Transportation/Washington, DC

State Departments of Commerce and Economic Development Councils/Washington, DC

Table 1.2 summarizes the primary equity sources just discussed.

Table 1.2
Capital Range of Primary Equity Sources

Source	Amount	Form
Stock market		
Private placements/ exempt offerings	$100,000+	Cash
Initial public offerings (IPOs)	$500,000–$1 million	Cash + Services
Employee Stock Option Plans (ESOPs)	Very Flexible	Cash + Services
Individuals		
Limited partnerships	$100,000+ if self- underwritten	Cash
Friends & family (F&F)	$0 to $100,000	Cash + Services
Corporations		
Joint ventures/licensing and technology transfer agreements	$50,000+	Cash + Services
Venture capital	$500,000; or $100,000 if incubator fund	Cash + Services
Partnerships	$50,000+	Cash + Services
Offshore Entities		
Merchant banks	$100,000 if qualified	Cash + Services
Individuals	$100,000+	Cash
Corporations	$100,000+	Cash

Financing Techniques to Access Debt Capital Sources

Commercial Lending

Most traditional bank debt, as well as loans from private lenders and other financial institutions, cost two or three percentage points above prime rate, depending on the geographical market and its relative economic health. In the 1980s, bank loans/lines of credit are among the most frequently tapped sources of capital for small businesses, primarily because entrepreneurs are unable to raise $100,000 or less from other debt or equity sources. It's difficult to get a small business loan under about $50,000; but in the $50,000 to $150,000 range, your chances get better. The problem isn't that loan capital is scarce or unavailable from banks, many large corporations, or financial institutions; the problem is that the borrowing qualifications for small business owners are getting more stringent.

In fact, some banks are demanding and getting stock warrants, in addition to the interest paid on the loan, as an equity kicker for assuming the added risks involved in a start-up or small venture. Look at it this way: Banks operate with a one-half of one percent profit margin, the national average, so they say they must be 99.5 percent safe in risking their capital in your company.

If you're willing to relocate the company to another country, debt capital is available from merchant banks all over the world. Nations like Holland and Ireland, for example, offer extensive loan programs that include tax reductions, land, plant/facilities, and many other corporate amenities, to U.S. firms that agree to set up shop in Europe, commit to building their local tax base through employment programs, and help enhance the local market infrastructure. These loans generally begin at about $100,000 and increase as you complete performance benchmarks. The merchant bank, which can be private or be an agency of the foreign government, usually also requires an equity participation in the form of warrants for stock or stock.

The U.S. Small Business Administration offers a myriad of lending programs designed for certain categories of small business owners, including minorities, women, the disadvantaged, and conservation specialists, among others. If you have fewer than 500 employees and you have been turned down by two local debt sources, you can borrow up to $150,000 on a direct loan from the SBA, $500,000 on a guaranteed loan (80 percent of the money is loaned by a commercial bank), $150,000 on a handicapped assistance loan and $500,000 on a Local Development Company loan. The SBA's Small Business Investment Company program offers regular loans, at rates slightly lower than the private markets, as well as equity capital of under $100,000 if your company has unusual growth potential.

Service/Manufacturing Companies: Most start-up service companies find it nearly impossible to get a loan except in the form of a small line of credit based on personal credit history.

Resource Possibilities: The Money Store/Local commercial banks

Asset-Based Lending (Finance Companies)

Since the 1970s, asset-based lenders (ABLs) have serviced a huge number of America's smallest companies that were considered too highly leveraged to get traditional commercial banking financing. ABLs provide funds in exchange for secured loans that are tailored to fit the current local economy. There are several forms of asset-based lending that share certain commonalities.

1. ABLs always secure your loan with collateral through Uniform Commercial Code security interest or by lender purchase of the asset, which can be accounts receivable or equipment, for example. The ABL allows the business to use the secured asset for a fee, similar to factoring and leasing.

2. ABLs nearly always specialize in specific financial services like factoring, leveraged buyouts or equipment financing.

3. ABLs get to know more about your company with a focused customer service strategy that addresses your specific financial requirements.

Four types of ABL are:

1. Working capital loans are advanced to provide cash to operate the business on a daily basis. The lender requires liquid assets like accounts receivable or inventory to secure this loan category. This is also called commercial finance lending outside the banking environment. A working capital loan is continuous, or not amortized, to provide daily funds; it may include different forms of term credit facilities even though the collateral may be less liquid, in the form of equipment or real estate.

2. Term loan facilities (term loans) are loans made independent of working capital and secured by fixed assets. Historically, they've been offered by independent finance companies known as *capital equipment lenders* because collateral was required in the form of machinery and equipment. They are usually repaid by periodic amortization in some form.

3. Receivables purchasing is another form of working capital loan. Accounts receivables are used as security for the loan, but you retain ownership and include them on your financial statements. Two other strategies, factoring and bulk receivable purchases, allow you to get the use of the cash tied up in your receivables. You sell the receivables to the lender. The receivable balances are carried on the lender's balance sheet after the transaction, because title has passed to the lender. *Factoring,* the purchase of accounts receivable, is the oldest form of asset-based lending. The factor owns the receivables, so he provides the required credit, collection, and accounting services to complete collection. The factor also assumes the risk of loss exposure, typically making individual credit decisions on each sale and resulting receivable. *Bulk purchases* are made on a nonnotification basis by large asset-based lenders to help large companies avoid hostile leveraged buyouts. (Many large firms with huge accounts receivables have been vulnerable to unfriendly takeover investors who use the company's

receivables as primary collateral in the LBO. Bulk purchases help these companies move their accounts receivable off the balance sheets.

4. Leasing is an outgrowth of the capital equipment financing market, with one difference: the finance company owns the equipment and leases it to the end-user, taking advantage of all tax benefits. A tax-driven strategy, the tax implications—and the unknown value of the equipment—confront the lessor at the end of the lease.

Service/Manufacturing Companies: By the nature of ABL, manufacturing and technology companies—which have specific assets in the form of tangible products and technologies—are financed most often by asset-based lenders.

Resource Possibilities: First Capital Corporation/Oklahoma City, OK

Limburg Investment Bank (LIOF)/Limburg Province, The Netherlands

Pooled Commercial Paper Issues

The commercial paper market is open to small business owners who want short-term (45-day) debt financing. Brokerage houses pool the commercial paper debt issue of several small companies for sale to larger corporations and institutional investors at interest rates that are 1 to 3 percent lower than prime rate.

The Benefit: Its short-term nature; you pay interest only for the period of time indicated by the issue, bypassing equity giveaways such as warrants for stock.

The Risk: Investors may fear your ability to repay debt if the market holds small issues in disfavor when interest rates are high. During those times, you may not be considered qualified for commercial paper debt, even though your loan is pooled with the loans of other small companies.

Service/Manufacturing Companies: Most pooled commercial paper funds prefer manufacturing/technology companies that have good credit ratings, rather than service companies for which credit often is unavailable in any form.

Resource Possibility: E.F. Hutton's Corporate Paper, Inc./New York City

Convertible (Hybrid) Securities

Convertible or hybrid securities are considered debt issues, although they contain an equity feature as a result of conversion toward the end of the payout period. Some convertible issues have been offered in the $70,000 to $80,000 range, although they are considered extremely small offerings. Most of these bond issues, even for small companies, begin at the $100,000 to $150,000 level. A new twist on convertibles is their appeal to certain foreign investors, usually groups of individuals or small offshore companies, that are willing to invest $100,000 to $500,000 in risk capital in exchange for ownership in a company that gives them a niche in a U.S. industry.

The Benefit: Their flexibility is a major benefit. They offer something for debt as well as equity investors, and the terms in both parts of the security offering can be equally flexible. Because some part of the loan reverts to valuable equity ownership, the interest rate you pay often is less than the two or three points above prime most entrepreneurs have to pay for debt financing. For you, they are a powerful tool to sweeten the deal for investors who may otherwise have considered your company too risky for investment purposes.

The Risk: Warrants for stock, on which you were depending for a later infusion of equity capital, may remain unexercised. Or your company's stock may not be valuable enough to entice reluctant debt investors. The offering must be staged carefully to insure that the exercise of the warrants provides the cash you need when you need it to pay off the loan.

Service/Manufacturing Companies: Because of the debt feature of convertible securities, service companies that lack dependable cash flow as well as salable assets are unlikely to be considered strong candidates for a hybrid offering.

Resource Possibility: Investment banks

Example: Lynn Reinner Publishers, Inc./Boulder, CO

Leveraged Buyout (LBO)

"Sons of LBOs," or scaled down versions of the famous hundred-million-dollar buyouts executed on Wall Street this decade, can be appropriate for small companies under certain circumstances. Many bank loans in the $100,000 to $200,000 range are variations of the LBO strategy, which lends funds to a buyout group—outside investors, family members, management—based on future cash flow and sometimes on the sale of assets (see Table 1.3).

The primary concern of lenders is that this debt strategy is supported by enough cash flow in your company to insure debt repayment by the new owners. Cash flow has become even more important than asset strength after double-digit interest rates early in the 1980s caused cash crises in many American corporations. To qualify for an LBO, you also need a solid and deep management team and a lot of growth potential in your industry. If you have a proprietary product, a dominant market position or a founder near retirement age, so much the better.

The Benefit: Cash availability for debt repayment. Banks and investment firms like buyouts because of the company's ready assets, which can be sold to pay off the bank loan. They also like the fact that the purchasers in a buyout, usually company managers or vendors, already are familiar with the operation. When interest rates are high and/or the new-issues market is soft, LBOs and other forms of mergers/buyouts bring high multiples in contrast to the replacement cost of a new company or product.

Service/Manufacturing Companies: Leveraged buyout lenders prefer manufacturing and technology companies over service

Table 1.3
Capital Range for Primary Debt Sources

Source	Range	Form
Stock market		
Convertible (hybrid) security	$100,000+	Cash from loan/warrants
Commercial paper	$100,000+	Cash
Lending institutions		
LBO	$100,000+	Cash from sale of assets
Bank loan	$100,000+	Cash/LOC
Offshore entities		
Merchant banking	$100,000	Cash + Services
Private market	$100,000	Cash

companies due to stringent loan qualifications that include lots of salable assets and enough cash flow to create an adequate multiple for interest coverage.

Resource Possibility: The Jordan Company/New York, NY

Example: Watkinson & Bournique/New York, NY

HOW TO CAPTURE INFLATIONARY AND RECESSIONARY TRENDS FOR YOUR FINANCING ADVANTAGE

Before you determine how much capital to raise, there is one more market parameter within which you should consider your financing request before you prepare the capital request: the economic condition and trends currently operative at the national and local levels (see Table 1.4).

Most of the time, the U.S. economy functions on a continuum between inflation at one pole and recession at the other pole.

Seldom does it hover at one extreme or the other, in a state of actual recession or inflation, for example. That's because the many entities and policies that affect the economy—the stock market, U.S. monetary policy, the Federal Reserve Board, cash in circulation, and many others—are in a constant state of motion. Every time you buy a share of stock, economic activity is affected to a proportionate degree; an FRB decision to devalue the dollar also has an effect, although it's proportionately greater. The day-to-day characteristic of the economy, therefore, should be viewed as constant movement along this continuum of inflation to recession.

The notion of movement in economic activity is helpful if you have ever tried to interpret newspaper and magazine articles about the condition and direction of the economy. Most business owners find it a difficult, if not impossible, task to assimilate conflicting articles and prognostications about what lies ahead and to apply what they read to their own companies. The task can be simplified for small businesses if you follow two guidelines: (1) apply the concept of movement—and degree of movement—to articles about economic indicators, and (2) concentrate only on the key indicators that affect the small business sector directly and immediately.

The stock market is affected directly and indirectly on a minute-to-minute basis by events such as a change in the unemployment rate, a large corporate bankruptcy, and assassination, that have very little, or no, direct effect on most small companies. The affects of these events usually merge into key economic indicators like interest rates if they are severe enough to reverse the present momentum of the market.

To keep it simple, evaluate only those indicators that have a direct and immediate impact on your business: the movement of interest rates; the trend in global export/import competition (tied to the strength of the dollar relative to other currencies); monetary policy changes if you export; and most important, the local and national trends in your industry.

To simplify even further, these indicators should become operative signals to you only when there is enough movement in any one of them to warrant a change in the way you run the business.

Table 1.4
Interpreting World Financial News

Headline	Inflationary Effect	Recessionary Effect
+Interest rate	Good news for equity financing until inflation rate falls; valuations higher; bad news for debt market.	Eventual negative effect on equity, but good news for debt market.
−Interest rate	Bad news for equity financing until inflation rate rises; valuations lower; good news for debt market.	Eventual positive effect on equity financing; good news for bonds.
War	Bad news for equity financing; valuations level off; good news for debt/bond market.	Good news for debt market and gold mine owners; valuations lower.
Foreign monetary changes	If currency rises against dollar, U.S. exports increase.	If currency falls against dollar, U.S. exports decrease.
Foreign competition	Stimulates equity financing and higher valuations; debt market declines.	Bad news for debt financing; capital flows overseas; valuations lower.

That means if interest rates are bouncing between only a one- or two-percentage point range and are not in the extremely high or low range, this indicator is not signaling you to make a change in the operation of your business or in your capital structure. If interest rates have gone up three points or more in the last six months, it's an inflationary signal that should be heeded: when inflationary effects are in play and still going up, equity financing is worth more, corporate valuations rise, and capital is easier to acquire. The reverse is true if interest rates decline by three or more points: when recessionary trends are evident and still going down, debt financing is worth more—but corporate valuations decline.

To make the trends work for you, look for two signals in the movement of the economic indicators that affect small business:

1. An indication of whether to ask for equity or debt, depending on the qualifications of your company

2. A guideline for planning later financing rounds

In the first signal, you want to solicit equity during growing inflationary movements and debt during declining recessionary movements. In the second signal, you want to plan future rounds of financing so that the capital needs of the company, for either debt or equity, coincide with the economic trend during the time of the financings. If a recession appears imminent for the quarter you plan another round of financing, the company should be ready and able financially to pay off additional debt service from a debt round of financing during that quarter.

Conversely, if inflation promises to emerge during the same quarter you plan a stock offering for equity capital, make sure there aren't too many shareholders who own overly diluted stock during that period. Keep an eye on what the investment analysts are recommending to their firms and to their clients. Newsletters that track investment trends are a great source of business ideas and indicate the general direction in which future capital is likely to flow. That's all you need. For example, the stock market now says forget the conventional wisdom of investing in food and clothing companies when the economy is inflationary. The new focus for undervalued stocks is in the pharmaceutical, utility, and healthcare sectors: they are all either inflation-proof or they pass along higher costs to customers. The most traditional hedge against inflation is still real estate. When inflation averaged 9.8 percent annually between 1978 and 1981, residential and commercial real estate yielded 17.7 percent returns annually, compared to 12.3 percent for stocks and −1.1 percent on T-bonds. One of the easiest and most convenient ways to hedge inflation, therefore, is with a limited partnership that invests in residential or commercial properties—despite the fact that they freeze your funds for up to 10 years and offer only passive tax advantages. In this inflationary scenario, investors will look for partnerships with a low risk level—that is, they pay cash for the properties instead of borrowing the purchase price—as well as immediate returns of 8 to 9 percent before the distribution to you as general partner is made. Remember that sophisticated investors will always evaluate your company's performance in periods of both high and low inflation.

IN SUMMARY

You are trying to identify the point in time (1) when you can get the highest value and price for equity financing—for your company valuation, for your stock, for your company—during inflationary trends, and (2) when you can pay the lowest interest rates for debt financing during recessionary trends (see Tables 1.5 and 1.6).

The key to knowing that point in time is difficult, even for the experts: to know when interest rates have peaked during inflation and when they have bottomed out during recession. But to maximize your financial request, it's imperative that you sell equity before and at the peak of rising interest rates, and to borrow capital before and at the bottom of a decline in interest rates to get the most money and value possible. That means the best time to ask for equity financing is when interest rates are still moving up and are short of their peak; the best time to ask for debt financing is when rates are still moving down and still short of their lowest point.

Table 1.5
Inflation/Recession Equity Financing

	Inflation Peak	Late Inflation	Recession Bottom	Late Inflation
Equity Strategy				
Private/exempt offering	Yes	No	No	No
IPO	Yes	No	No	No
Limited partnership	Yes	No	No	No
Venture capital	Yes	No	No	No
Merger/buyout	Yes	No	No	No
F&F	Yes	No	No	No
ESOP	Yes	No	No	No
Joint venture	Yes	No	Maybe	No
Licensing agreement	Yes	No	Maybe	No
Corporate partnership	Yes	No	Maybe	No

When interest rates have peaked and start down again, recessionary effects begin to show and your financing strategy should change to debt: there is less demand for money because it has finally become expensive and scarce after the inflationary glut, so interest rates fall; if there is stiff global competition, capital becomes even more scarce because it flows toward imports; if the dollar is expensive compared to other currencies, fewer people buy your products.

When interest rates have bottomed out and start up again, inflationary effects emerge and your financing strategy should change to equity: there is more demand for money, corporate valuations rise, and stock prices rise; if global competition is down, inflation is supported even further.

It's vitally important that you acquire relevant and updated information about the local and national trends in your industry, particularly in low-, medium-, and high-technology industries. When an industry trend is pervasive enough, it can sway not only the conditions within which your company operates,

Table 1.6
Inflation/Recession Debt Financing

	Inflation Peak	Late Inflation	Recession Bottom	Late Recession
Debt Strategy				
Hybrid security	No	No	Yes	No
Bank lending	No	No	Yes	No
Debenture	No	No	Yes	No
Commercial paper	No	No	Yes	No
LBO	No	No	Yes	No

but also the entire public market for all small companies. In late 1988, a major softening in the computer industry, plus the fear of rising interest rates, made it nearly impossible for small companies in any industry to raise money in the new-issues market. ComputerLand Corporation canceled an initial public offering scheduled for August, 1988 because of the precipitous decline in stock prices in the computer industry. That same month, Wyse Technology postponed indefinitely a secondary offering of 1.7 million shares for the same reason. The result was that the fear of rising interest rates lowered the demand for new technology stock because the computer industry is capital- intensive. It was perceived that customers of computer companies often need to borrow money to pay for big-ticket items such as computer systems; and the companies themselves would find additional borrowing expensive in that economic scenario.

It's important that you acquire background information about your industry so that your financial analysis is thorough. The other reason to gather industry statistics is that investors who review your financing package are likely to counter your capital request—and your blue-sky projections of sales and earnings—with its own documentation, from such organizations as the Council on Competitiveness. Its 1988 report cited the following developments in U.S. business:

- American companies' share of the U.S. market has shrunk dramatically in many technology fields. Between 1970 and 1987, U.S. manufacturing companies' share of the American market in phonographs fell from 90 to 1 percent; in color televisions from 90 to 10 percent; in machine tools from 100 to 35 percent, and in telephones from 99 to 25 percent according to the report.

- Foreign inventors captured 47 percent of U.S. patents in 1987, up from 35 percent in 1975, with Japanese inventors holding key patents in an increasing number of fields.

- By 1986, Japan had captured 65 percent of the world market in computer chips. The United States had less than 30 percent of that market.

Equity investors will understand your business more thoroughly if you have enough information to chart comparable public companies as shown in Table 1.7.

Table 1.7
Companies with the Highest Monthly Stock Gain by Industry

	Drug Mfr. Jones Med. Ind. (JMED/ NASDAQ)	*Computers* Tigera Gp. (TYGR/ NASDAQ)	*Electronics* Old Dominion (ODSI/ NASDAQ)
Earnings/share			
Last quarter	.09	.00	.03
1-yr. change	28.6	NE*	.00
P/E ratio	20.0	NE	NE
Debt/equity ratio	.09	.01	.31
Latest 12-mo. rev.	$7.2 million	$500,000	$8 million

Source: "Leading 100," *High Technology Business,* September, 1988
*NE = negative earnings

THE BOTTOM-LINE FORMULA FOR RAISING A SMALL AMOUNT OF CAPITAL

Now that you have reviewed the decision points for structuring a capital request, consider the small business financing rule of thumb as it functions in actual practice: Raising $100,000 is harder to raise than $1 million. The $100,000 level is perceived as a psychological barrier by many capital sources as well as by many investors in the private market. If you want to make the funding job easier, justify the need for $200,000 or $300,000 by adapting another rule of thumb used by start-up financiers. The old rule is: Triple your expenses and halve your revenue. The rule for start-up owners who want to break the $100,000 barrier is: Double your expenses as well as your revenue.

The key to making this adaptation work, however, is hard evidence that your growth potential can support these projections. The best way to back up the projections is to provide due diligence on industry standards and competitors—local and national—and to convince investors that your management team has quality, perseverance, a track record, breadth, and depth. If you can produce the backup for a $200,000 or $300,000 financial request instead, the number and kind of capital sources you can access won't increase so much as investor interest level, degree of participation, and ease of selling your deal will. In addition, the public market will be more responsive to your company if your request exceeds even $200,000.

CHAPTER 2

Preparing the Financial Package

▶ **Capital Request:** A request upfront in the business plan or financial package, usually in the Executive Summary, for a specific amount of equity or debt financing. The request is repeated and amplified in the financial section.

▶ **Cash Out (Exit):** The strategy by which management and investors can get out of the investment with a profit, often in the form of extra returns (ROI), proceeds from the sale of the company, or of cash from the sale of insider shares in an initial public offering.

▶ **Growth:** Growth may mean 10 to 20 percent annual increases in revenue or earnings to you, but it means more to many investors. To venture capitalists, for example, growth means taking the company to five to 10 or more times initial size in three to five years. Determine what growth means to an equity or debt source before you describe what a good deal your investment is to that source.

▶ **Key Ratios:** The ratios sophisticated investors look to first to determine the health of your company's financial infrastructure, particularly lenders, including the debt/equity, current, inventory turnover, and receivable turnover ratios. Always compare your key ratios to industry standards, if available, to project how healthy your company looks to investors in comparison with competitors. (Key ratios are defined in greater detail in this chapter.)

▶ **Market Research:** The professional study of your geographical and customer markets, potential markets, the regulatory and tax environments, the competition, the economic environment within which your company operates, the marketing and distribution systems that will reach target markets, and population/buying trends. Although many entrepreneurs conduct their own, informal market research using neighborhood networks, customer query, and experience, investors prefer market research that has been thoroughly and realistically compiled by professional marketing or consulting firms.

▶ **Seat-of-the-Pants (SOP) Management:** An aggressive, goal-oriented approach to operating a business characterized by centralized authority, one-way communication, personalized organizational structure, and a technically based owner (compared to a professional management style characterized by decentralized authority, two-way communication, formal organizational structure, and a management-specialist owner.

The preparation of the financial package—the business plan with a built-in financing strategy for raising debt or equity capital—is the most important first step in raising money successfully. Forget the idea that you can impress a venture capitalist out of millions by scrawling a business plan on the back of a cocktail napkin. Too many entrepreneurs are chasing too few dollars these days for that to work. Investors have become much more sophisticated and knowledgeable about your industry than they used to be, so it is as much their rules as yours that determine how the financing package should be developed. The best financing packages are those thought out and written to answer a specific investor's most probing questions. As you begin to prepare the package, your mindset should be: What does this investor want to know about my company, my product, and me? In what form should I give him as much relevant data as possible? In what order? How does he want to exit? How fast with how much?

A financing package that hits the mark and raises money has certain components that are of keen interest to both debt and equity investors in the public and private markets. They should be included in every financing package and then "steered" to the appropriate capital source with a cover letter upfront. The components are:

- Cover letter
- Executive summary
- Table of contents
- Company description and history
- Corporate growth strategy
- Market research, analysis, and strategy
- Technology/R&D analysis
- Manufacturing/operations plan
- Sales strategy

- Management
- Organization/personnel
- Financial plan
- Financial data
- Appendices

Before you begin to prepare the financing document, it is help-ful to review what venture capitalists and bankers really want from the entrepreneurs they invest in—what they consider win-ning qualities. If you can infuse your financing request with evi-dence that you possess these qualities and then apply them to the components listed above, you will be more likely to get the cash you need:

- An entrepreneur who is committed to the venture: A winner is persistent, not easily defeated, and has a large percent of net worth tied up in the company.

- An entrepreneur who is capable of allocating limited re-sources: A winner has good judgment, is focused, and keeps effective control.

- An entrepreneur who produces what is promised: A winner is results-oriented, is hard on self and others to achieve the corporate mission, and is highly energetic.

- An entrepreneur who keeps the venture capitalist/banker in-formed: A winner is honest and provides timely information such as monthly financials and operating reports, and yearly audited financials and operations/budget plans.

Venture Capitalist	Banker

Cover Letter

This should be a personalized letter directed to a specific person by name and title. It is the first page of the package, appearing even before the Table of Contents. The letter should outline in less than one page why you are sending the document to this person, why your investment opportunity is a good venture capital deal and how you plan to follow up the solicitation. The letter can be standardized for all venture capital sources, and even some private investors who use the more stringent evaluation methods used by venture firms. The letter also should point out where in the package the venture capitalist can quickly locate the key data he wants to evaluate: revenue/income projections, assumptions, and exit strategies, among other factors. Although it can be a form letter for the venture capital industry, every letter should be addressed personally.

Cover Letter

This letter can be standardized for most debt investors and financial institutions with few changes. Personalize the letter to a specific banker or debt investor by name and title, and change the emphasis on the financial data to highlight what you know this lender wants to evaluate: cash flow, collateral, and existing debt service, among other factors.

Executive Summary

This section may be the first, last, and only chance you have to get the attention of a venture capitalist. Venture firms receive so many business plans and financing packages that many venture capitalists take the time to read only the executive summaries. That means you have from two to six pages to make your story count with a venture capitalist. Less than 10 percent of

Executive Summary

Bankers are more likely to read your financing package more thoroughly than venture capitalists do, but they look for the same data and financial highlights in the Executive Summary. In particular, a banker looks for some measurement of cash flow and assets in this section to whet his appetite for the big picture further back in the document.

Venture Capitalist

the plans an investor reads passes this first review, so the decision to read your entire plan is made in the first five minutes. The executive summary should emphasize the key points in the plan, a brief outline and description of your company, your products/services/technology, and a definition of the marketplace where you will do business. It should delineate who and where the market is and what is happening in the market to create a need for your products. It positions the company among the competition. Include a glimpse of the overall finance picture of your company, with any history of earnings as well as a forecast of future earnings. Add a management profile with appropriate descriptions of why you and your management team/employees are best able to run this company.

Table of Contents

After the venture capitalist's interest has been piqued by the Executive Summary, he or she will turn first to the Table of Contents to find the location of specific information in the document.

This table should be organized in a format that is recognizable by and comfortable to local venture capitalists; do not get creative with the sequence of the information in the package. Usually, a venture investor wants to review your people, your markets, your competitive health

Banker

Table of Contents

The banker will want to review the management team/owners and the financial data first, so these headings should be clearly identified. Bankers, like venture capitalists, believe that the management team must possess the professional expertise and personal qualities required to build a company. Make debt lenders happy by subheading the components of the financial section to include income and profit/loss statements, pro formas and assumptions.

Venture Capitalist

and environment, and your company's areas of distinction and competence first. If the document includes illustrations, photographs, charts, or other artwork, it is helpful to include a Table of Contents for the artwork apart from the table that locates the narrative and financial data.

Company Description and History

This section can be the most difficult of all to write. A good exercise is to sum up the precise nature of the business in one paragraph. Many entrepreneurs find it an impossible task, which is a signal to rethink the whole concept. If the nature of the business isn't absolutely clear in one paragraph, it will be difficult to persuade investors that you can create success in a marketplace where your competitors know just where they are going.

This section should include the major products/services/technology and their applications. It's the section to show investors how well you sell: Be sure to toot your own horn by identifying the special competence of your product and how that will help sell it successfully, especially if you are in a competitive industry or market, or you are a start-up operation with no earnings history. Explain what new element your product brings to the marketplace and what unrecognized need it fulfills. Explain to investors why your window of opportunity is

Banker

Company Description and History

Debt investors will probably look at management's expertise and track record, and the company's financial picture first. Your salesmanship counts heavily with bankers, too: They want to be convinced in this section that management is the very best leadership for the company, that it has a track record in the company's industry and that it has steered the company successfully toward the goals that were established at inception. In broad strokes, also emphasize for debt investors the overall financial health of the company. Highlight any history of earnings, as well as forecasts of future earnings. Many bankers like to see a capsule of worst-case and best-case scenarios, or a range of possibilities in this section.

Venture Capitalist

Banker

open now. This section should answer the most important question a venture capitalist will ask: If the achievement of success is complex, do the rewards outweigh the risks? Double the importance of this question for a start-up company. This question requires a detailed, clear explanation of how you will succeed if a market doesn't exist yet, and if the sales and distribution channels must be created. The historical analysis, particularly if the company is more than one year old, should include general information about the founding, the founding team, and the corporate structure. If you are incorporated, disclose information about corporate stock classes, the number of shares outstanding, and about warrants and options. Explain how equity is distributed, who has invested capital, and the general direction of the company. This is the real question in this section: Is the company on track, doing what it said it would do?

Corporate Growth Strategy

To succeed in a competitive and increasingly global marketplace, your product/service/technology should fill a need perceived by your target markets. The need you fill automatically creates a position or niche for your product, which can be anything from a lower price, a superior method of delivery, or a higher level of quality to geographical

Corporate Growth Strategy

A banker will not consider what your corporate growth strategy, or positioning strategy, is so much as how well management has retained the company's position in the marketplace. This means a banker considers it management's job to determine the appropriate niche for the company and its products; the investor will determine how well

Venture Capitalist	**Banker**

expansion, a merger or acquisition, or the addition of new products to your current product line. High-tech products, which are appealing to many high-risk venture capitalists, often must be sold to a market that is created or educated as the product is sold. The positioning strategy for corporate growth must be outlined in extra detail by companies in cutting-edge, emerging, or nonexistent industries.

you have taken your place in the market. To a banker, your positioning strategy is a measurement of how well you do what you set out to do. Make sure you demonstrate that you are and have been controlling company operations effectively.

Market Research, Analysis, and Strategy

Venture capitalists consider every business to be market driven. If success results from sales to the marketplace, a detailed knowledge of the marketplace is essential to the successful entrepreneur. Here, venture capitalists look for your level of understanding about all of the marketplace factors that affect your sales; a high level of understanding indicates to investors that you have the capability of making complex and conflicting decisions about business. First, provide a full background of your industry, including its size, chief characteristics, trends, and your major customers—today, in five years, in ten years. Explain the applications of your product and how they may change in time. Project actual and potential changes inside and outside the industry that will impact your business at different points in time. Describe your

Market Research, Analysis, and Strategy

A lender will be interested in the same market highlights, but with a different twist: Because market strategies, by necessity, are still blue-sky projections, he will concentrate on the quality of the documentation provided by professional research, by management's track record and by existing sales. The projections may look conservative, the marketplace may look inviting, but how close to reality are the projections? A banker also will be interested in the macro factors that could have a direct effect on cash flow, including cheap foreign competition, a downturn in the economy, or changing regulatory requirements. Of special interest to a banker are the sales and operations of your competition.

Venture Capitalist   **Banker**

target markets and give realistic
assumptions about market
share—now and in one year and
five years. One of the biggest mistakes entrepreneurs make in this
section is to predict how much
the company will sell based on
general numbers for the size of
the market. The real question
here is: Who will buy *your*
product and why? A bottom-up
analysis based on sales projections using specific customers is
more credible than a percent of a
general market. Then document
your reasoning with professional
marketing research, either from
a research consulting firm or
in-house with the help of trade
associations and government
statistics. Most venture capitalists shy away from investing in
companies that are crowded by
more than 5 or 10 competitors.
Describe your competition, compare their products to yours, and
outline your strategies to sell
more than they do. Explain how
difficult or easy it is to compete
against you and how you distribute your products. One of the
easiest ways to determine your
position in the marketplace relative to the competition is to use a
matrix. List the top 10 features
of your product on the horizontal
axis and list competitors below
your name on the vertical axis.
Rank the features from one (lowest rating) to ten (highest rating).
Then explain how much budget
you have to advertise and promote the product, and outline

Venture Capitalist   **Banker**

specific marketing activities for promoting your company and product to specific target markets. Get a reaction to your product from specific customers; you can bet that a potential investor will perform due diligence on your product, so you should know first how your customers regard you.

Technology and Research and Development

This section is another primary focus for venture capitalists, who want to know the basic idea behind the technology, to see a working prototype, and to review a production run, if applicable. They will typically demand a patent or copyright on the process or product, and the range of protection possible for expanding the patent rights. The venture capitalist's question here is: Are patents an effective way to protect the company's technology? Usually a hidden component or secret ingredient is added to the technology to create a more effective barrier to entry than a patent can provide. At issue here, also, is the depth of detail you should reveal in the description of your technology. Although most professionals in the industry do not disclose trade secrets, some patent rights have been lost to unethical venture capitalists who passed on the information in your plan to competitors and other venture capitalists. Further, you need to describe

Technology and Research and Development

Because of the risk inherent in a technology or process that has not been commercialized, most bankers don't finance the high-tech or R&D sector of small business. Minus cash flow, usually minus collateral of any kind except certain ownership rights to the technology, is little incentive to invest for the lender who wants security in exchange for his investment. Even if the technology or process has been commercialized in the form of a licensing or technology transfer agreement, it will take more than signed contracts to wrest financing from a banker.

Venture Capitalist

what available technology is superior or equal to yours, how marketable and how creative competitive technology is, and what products you will R&D for future sales. Venture capitalists look for a product line to result directly from the first-generation product.

Manufacturing and Operations Plan

This plan describes how you will accomplish production or conduct service operations: How much will you complete internally and by what methods, and how much will you subcontract at the start and after two years? The venture capitalist is looking for your operating advantages here. What is the nature of your facility and how high is the quality level? Be sure to include descriptions of plant and office space, equipment and machinery, storage and land. If your company is a start-up, detail how you plan to put a manufacturing facility together, with what resources. Also include such factors as proposed expansion, distance to customers, vendors and backups for emergencies, worker training and/or access to a skilled labor pool, the effect of state and local laws on your facility, inventory management, setting quality and production controls, and the bidding process you plan to use. What documentation supports your decisions about these manufacturing

Banker

Manufacturing and Operations Plan

The banker will be interested in the same manufacturing elements, but he will translate them into measurements of how well you manage your margins. One of his primary concerns is controlling, or at least knowing, all possible production costs: the firmer your control of costs, the more reliable your revenue and earnings projections tend to be.

Venture Capitalist   **Banker**

elements? Most important, the
venture capitalist will want to
know the standard production
costs at different volume levels
and how overhead, labor, material costs, and the cost of parts
will affect production costs. Outline the capital requirements,
how costs are recovered and the
time period.

Debt Financing Request: What Investors Want to Know

The Request:
Purpose
Amount
Terms
Repayment source
Available collateral

The Business:
Succinct description
Projected changes

The Management:
Age, experience, education
Key personnel and outside advisors

The Operations:
Products
Markets/distribution
Customers
Suppliers
Competition
Facilities
Employees/unions

The Finances:
Three years of annual balance
   sheets and income statements
Three years of tax returns
Ratio analysis with appropriate
   comments

Venture Capitalist   **Banker**

The Finances: *(continued)*

Personal financial statements of
principals, dated within 90 days
of request

Pro forma income statement for at
least one year

Pro forma balance sheet for at least
one year

Cash budget for at least one year

Resource Possibility: David E.
Eikner, Colorado National Bank,
Denver, CO

Sales Strategy

This section demonstrates to a
venture capitalist your ability to
transform a business idea into a
profit-making business. Ideally,
it outlines all of the steps you will
take to reach your sales goals and
it will serve as a master skeleton
for a more detailed marketing
plan later on. This section covers
your distribution methods, geographical penetration, rollout
schedule and locations, sales ratings, and promotional assistance.
Also covered is one of the most
important decisions you will
make: the pricing structure,
which must make your product
competitive and yet generate
profits. In terms of actual selling,
you must identify prospective
customers and decision-makers,
decide how to contact them and
in what order, and determine the
type of sales force and the level of
sales effort you will expect.
Describe the sales compensation
system, the selling cycle for

Sales Strategy

A debt investor, particularly a
banker, will be most interested in
the human cost of sales in this
part of the equation. It is a good
idea to substantiate your estimates of selling costs by relating
yours to industry standards for
commission structures, salaries
and draws, expense accounts, and
other related sales expenses.
Again, bankers will try to gauge
how familiar you are with the
cost of selling in your industry
and how well you control this
ratio in your own company.

Venture Capitalist	**Banker**

your product, and the sales milestones. Then document your evaluations to support these estimates.

Management

It has been said of the venture capital industry that the only thing it looks for in a potential investment is "management, management, management." That may not be the only factor, but it is very important to investors whose primary job is to determine which managers have what it takes to become successful for themselves and for the company. No matter how receptive the market is or how distinctive the product, it takes outstanding people to start up and manage a company for profitable growth. Venture capitalists look for a well-rounded management team that has complementary strengths. All the key positions are filled; there is a visionary CEO at the helm, a financial expert, a marketing manager, a technical expert, and a motivated production head. It's more reassuring to venture investors when the management team has prior experience in the same industry and a solid track record. If you lack a track record, reference a good education and previous outstanding jobs and accomplishments. Also in this section are a description of key managers, a strategy for attracting and compensating them, a salary scale, and a description of

Management

Bankers do as much due diligence of their own on the members of your management team as they do on your balance sheet and income statement. Be assured that your character and past business associations will be reviewed carefully before a loan is extended. If you haven't provided enough background information, such as references, client names, or previous lenders, it will be requested of you.

Venture Capitalist	**Banker**

how the credentials of key managers meet the company's needs. Describe your staffing needs now and in one year, list who has outstanding, noncompete employment contracts, indicate who is on the board of directors, and explain how qualified investors could fit with the company's board or its management structure.

Organization and Personnel

In competitive industries, investors look for strategies that will attract and keep managers and employees who have other employment opportunities with the competition. Include salary, stock, and/or profit-sharing compensation methods; "golden handcuff" options; recognition programs, or special awards and merits; publishing opportunities for the technical staff; and companywide beer bashes or softball teams. Describe the career path potential for technical and administrative staff and management. Chart the current organizational structure and project the structure in two years. Most investors will want a list of current stockholders and their holdings by number of shares, and an indication of the amount of stock currently authorized and issued.

Organization and Personnel

Debt investors will be concerned primarily with the status of their debt investment relative to the equity investors. In other words, is the loan subordinated? Which equity investments will be paid before their debt is repaid? For this reason, the amount of stock available to employees through stock option plans and profit-sharing programs, for example, is reviewed carefully.

Financial Plan

This is a key section indicating how much capital you want to raise and at what stages in the

Financial Plan

Bankers say there are three things to watch in a small business: cash, cash, and cash. Unlike

Venture Capitalist

company's development. It includes your analysis of the company's debt/equity ratio, a detailed use of funds section, deferred payments explanation, and your valuation of the company. List the terms you prefer, an approximate per-share price, and potential dilution. Equity investors will consider highly important your projection of the company's valuation, level of liquidity, and ability to attract financing options when the company needs another round of money. If you can grow the company to $15 million or $20 million in five years, most equity investors will be interested in your project. To clinch their interest, explore exit options in detail. Many investors look for a company that is a strong candidate for an initial public offering or sale to increase the value of their investments.

Financial Data

Expect to provide historical financial statements for the past three to five years, including balance sheets, profit and loss statements, and current financial statements. Add monthly or quarterly profit/loss and cash flow projections for three to five years or until breakeven—then add these projections on an annual basis for five years. Many venture capitalists also require current monthly statements for the first year, quarterly statements for the next two years, and

Banker

venture capitalists, they don't want to see rapid growth because growth threatens cash. If you're not a venture capital candidate, include a pro forma profit and loss statement that ties to your sales forecast a pro forma cash flow statement and a pro forma balance sheet. One easy way to prepare the numbers is to make a realistic, 90-day forecast and multiply by four, taking into account any seasonal fluctuations in the business. Then adjust the numbers every quarter. Also calculate a breakeven analysis to tell you and your banker what kind of volume you need to stay ahead of the game. Very important: Describe in detail how the debt investor will be repaid.

Financial Data

Project how a banker will view your financing package by analyzing key ratios before you make the capital request. Projections aside, he will always emphasize the ratios that show how well your cash cycle meshes with your operational cycle, and that show past performance over future performance. (1) Current ratio: It is total current assets divided by total current liabilities. This tells a banker how well you meet current liabilities as they come due. Companies with low inventory

Venture Capitalist	**Banker**

then annual statements for two or three years. Also include balance sheet forecasts for the end of each year, capital budgets and the manufacturing/distribution plan. Pay particular attention to your cash flow projections, which indicate how well your financing is timed, and which track the types of financing and repayment terms you have already committed to. Investors will review your balance sheet for the debt/equity ratio, the amounts of available working capital, and the inventory turnover rate. Project two or three scenarios for the company's performance in a strong, weak, and neutral economy. Your analysis also should be based on two different debt and equity assumptions. Identify breakeven clearly, as well as the market value of the company based on a price/earnings ratio of similar companies. Make sure the assumptions underlying your pro formas are well documented and geared to industry standards, for such things as: the accounting method used, sales and market share, accounts receivable, R&D costs, state and federal taxes, interest and payroll expenses, and materials costs. Occasionally, a venture capitalist or other equity investor will ask you to rework the numbers using different assumptions or a different set of numbers.

and strict credit policies usually can operate safely with a lower current ratio than companies with easy credit and a greater proportion of current assets in inventory. (2) Debt/equity ratio: It is total liabilities divided by total stockholders' equity (net worth). Bankers like this ratio because it compares what's owed to what's owned. It measures your company's financial leverage. The higher the ratio, the greater the leverage and the greater your profitability if sales increase; high leverage is riskier if sales decline. High leverage should indicate to you that future borrowing might be expensive or even unavailable. (3) Receivable turnover ratio: it is net sales on account divided by average receivable balance. Bankers use this to determine the relationship between your volume of credit business and average outstanding receivables. A higher turnover indicates a shorter collection period and better collectibility of accounts receivable. If you divide 360 days by this receivable turnover rate, you'll get the average number of days it takes to collect accounts receivable. Other key ratios include inventory turnover (annual cost of sales divided by average inventory) and return on equity (net income divided by net worth).

If you operate a service business, narrate a marketing strategy in the financial request based on

Venture Capitalist	**Banker**

the way these factors function in your business as shown in Figure 2.1.

In the operation cycle represented on the debit side of the balance sheet, cash is utilized to buy or produce inventory which is sold and the resultant receivables eventually collected. In the financing cycle, represented on the credit side of the balance sheet, cash is furnished through accounts payable to suppliers or notes payable to other creditors such as banks. Cash is the pivotal point, the gear where the two cycles mesh.

Appendices

Although some venture capitalists require that a copy of the patent be included in this section, it is not considered prudent to share proprietary information about your technology or product in such detail with investors who lack the technical expertise to understand the data. Other exhibits which should be placed here include a board of directors list, management/ owner resumes, market studies, professional references, trade journal articles and/or pictures of the product or prototype.

Appendices

In addition to the appendices mentioned in the venture capitalist version of this section, you may want to include extra financial data or more detailed support/documentation for your decisions in this version for debt investors.

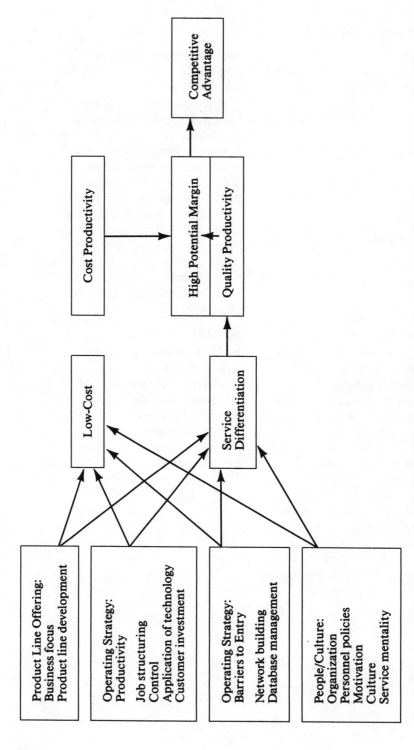

Figure 2.1 Important Relationships That Build Competitive Advantage in Service Companies

Source: David Heskett, "Managing in the Service Economy," Harvard Business School Press, 1986. Used with permission.

CHAPTER 3

Investigating Primary Sources of Capital

▶ **Bridge Financing:** A short-term loan usually granted in anticipation of longer-term financing from an outside source.

▶ **(Management) Buyout:** The management purchase of a controlling percentage of a company's stock, via a tender offer or negotiation, in order to assume ownership of corporate operations and assets.

▶ **Equity Kicker:** A sweetener or inducement to investors to buy an equity position along with the debt investment, such as a convertible bond or debenture with (performance) warrants.

▶ **Exit:** The strategy by which management and/or investors cash out of an investment, for example, merger, IPO, or buyout before or after it turns profitable.

▶ **Insurance Companies:** Many small to medium-sized insurance companies now book their own deals at competitive rates as aggressively as large insurance companies have for decades. They look for "yield enhancement vehicles" like private placements for equity participation, rather than investing in debt deals exclusively through brokerage house syndicates.

▶ **Leveraged Buyout (LBO):** The takeover of a company by insiders or outsiders using corporate assets as collateral for the loan to finance the transaction. The acquiring group repays the loan out of corporate cash flow. This strategy often is used to take the company private.

▶ **Mezzanine Financing:** Late-round financing preparatory to a public offering.

▶ **Offering Circular (Placement Memorandum, Prospectus):** A formal, written offer to sell shares used in such offerings as an initial public offering, private placement, and limited partnership, among others. It discloses all details about a proposed or existing business so that potential investors can make an informed investment decision.

▶ **Public Markets:** Potential stock buyers/sellers among the public at large; these markets can be accessed with IPOs, secondary offerings, limited partnerships, blind pool deals, or warrants, among other offerings.

▶ **Return on Investment (ROI):** The percent amount earned on a company's total capital, calculated by dividing total capital into earnings before interest, taxes, and dividends. It can be used to compare companies or departments within a company, measuring management efficiency, and product justification.

FRIENDS AND FAMILY

Forms

The Handshake

The informal financial relationship built on a handshake is the cheapest source of equity around: friends and family, or F&F as it's called in the venture capital industry. You can raise several hundred to many thousands of dollars in the F&F market, generally on a short-term basis when the company first begins operations. With no strings attached, F&F generates cheap capital to use for everything from the incorporation fee to equipment, inventory, and occasionally your salary. F&F capital usually doesn't take long to get, you don't have to spend a lot of money to get it, and it doesn't generate a lot of paperwork. But maybe it should. Without a contract specifying investment terms and the intentions of both parties, this relationship can cause endless problems that are exacerbated by friendly and familial ties.

The Formal Contract

Most small-business management consultants, accountants, and attorneys recommend that an F&F relationship to the company should be legalized by a formal contract that regards family and friends the same way outside investors are regarded: carefully and respectfully. The contract should state the amount of capital advanced, the form of returns expected by family and friends, their legal relationship to the company, and the ramifications of nonperformance by either party are the most important terms to include in an F&F contract. Many entrepreneurs pare down a standard investor contract for a simplified, inexpensive document that will serve the same purpose.

A Family Business

When an F&F relationship becomes significant in terms of dollars, expertise, or sweat equity, it is time to decide if the company has become an unofficial family business. If your children have worked there every summer for 10 years, or the sales department wouldn't function without your best friend in the manager's office, or Aunt Mary still "invests" $5,000 every time you need a loan, it may be time to formalize everyone's relationship to the business, including such thorny family-business issues as: right of succession to chief executive officer; inheritance apportionment among offspring; and chain of command before, during, and after a new succession to CEO.

Example: Ricardo's Gourmet Foods, Inc./Houston

Resource Possibility: The Center for Family Business/Cleveland, OH

Investor Markets

Family Members

The best way to approach a family member, preferrably one who has discretionary cash available, is to make individual solicitations and treat him or her like an outside investor. Make an effort to capsulize the business, the product, the market, the competition, and the projections. Keep the projections simple and realistic; don't ask for more than you can repay or turn into profits. Be willing and able to explain how "family investors" will cash out, how much they will get, the timeframe for returns or repayment, and the amount of personal equity you have in the business. Be prepared to discuss how much participation you feel is acceptable from family investors, some of whom may feel that their investment in you grants certain decision-making privileges in your company. If they are reluctant to invest, don't press the issue. A reluctant family investor can turn into a very dissident shareholder in a year or two, if your solicitation is accepted under pressure. Take yourself, and the business, seriously.

Nearly Family

These are people with whom you have close, personal relationships and for that reason should put under contract for the investment, including spouses, best friends, mentors, and anyone you socialize with regularly.

Professional Colleagues

The best prospects are people you know professionally from a previous job, a professional association, a civic committee, or any business organization. These people know you in a corporate context and they are more likely to understand the financial requirements of starting up a new company. Take the time to prepare an informal proposal describing the company, the product, the market, the competition, and the projections. Show how much return they'll get and when. When you receive your first F&F cash infusion, use that reference to get other friends and family members interested in your business. Along with professional colleagues, consider distant friends, acquaintances, service people, and vendors as F&F markets.

Requirements

The investor requirements of an F&F financing are relatively easy to satisfy as long as they have been delineated clearly, preferrably in a contract, before you receive the cash or distribute returns. Most F&F investors prefer a cash return on investment (ROI) if their contribution is considered equity. The ROI typically is lower than what outside investors expect, sometimes as low as 5 to 10 percent for an investment of $10,000 or less. They prefer a minority interest in your company (although some family members or friends may change their minds later), therefore, they won't demand management participation or a seat on your board of directors unless you solicit these services. F&F financing allows you, for the most part, to determine your own gestation period before which the investment doesn't have to be cashed out. These investors are not concerned about planning a more permanent exit from the company in terms of initial investment once they receive their returns, assuming their contribution has been less than 50 percent of the equity in the company.

Most F&F investors want to be wooed just like any other outside investor—with a business plan and well-reasoned assumptions underlying your projections of corporate growth. That means you should at least review the standard investor requirements with them: Projected sales and earnings levels, prospects and markets, management strength, company position in the industry, ability to capitalize the company in the future, and personal commitment to all aspects of operations. The difference is that F&F investors won't scrutinize these elements of success as closely as outside investors will. They allow you more room and more time to make mistakes.

The financing requirements of F&F versus IPO are compared in Table 3.1.

Table 3.1
F&F Financing Requirements

Requirements	F&F	IPO
Method of return	Cash/ROI	Cash/stock profits
Ownership	Minority	Majority
Board seat	No	Yes
Maturity	You decide	Immediate growth
Exit	N/A	Public stock sale
Track record	No	Yes
Sales/earnings standards by industry	No	Yes
Management depth	No	Yes
Industry niche	No	Yes
Growth potential	Minimal	Maximum

Offshore Potential

Most F&F investments are so small—usually no more than $25,000—that there is little margin after covering current liabilities and accounts payable to expand or penetrate overseas markets.

Third-Party Professionals

Attorneys

A law firm should be engaged to write an investor contract or review a contract you've adapted for that purpose. The contract should be signed by all family members and/or friends who have agreed to invest even a small amount of capital in your company.

Accountants

Financial record-keeping becomes more important as the company grows. Because you'll be required to produce audited financial records at some stage of development—for such purposes as selling a private placement offering or merging with a larger corporation—it is a good idea to hire a professional accounting firm as soon as you can afford it. Audited financials provide the most convincing documentation when investor disputes arise; they're even more important when the investors are friends and family.

Costs

There are virtually no costs involved in raising F&F capital except the interest expense on a loan or the returns guaranteed in exchange for equity. Occasionally, F&F investors require other trade-offs in exchange for their backing.

Action Plan to Access F&F Financing

One Month Ahead

Prepare a two- to three-page proposal letter for F&F investors which describes the company, the product, the market, the competition, and growth projections. Use a simple, straightforward letter style, and keep the projections realistic.

Two Weeks Ahead

With family and friends, it is important to convey serious intent. Call each potential investor in advance for an appointment, just as an outside investor should be contacted.

How to Time F&F Financing

Macroeconomic indicators like the U.S. monetary policy, the imbalance of trade, and action taken by the Federal Reserve Board won't have a direct impact on the amount or quality of capital available from the friends-and-family market. First, the effects of many of these indicators don't trickle down to the small business sector until after a 6-month or 12-month lag time has elapsed. Second, F&F financing usually isn't based on economics anyway: this market makes an investment based on personal relationship with you, rather than on the merits of your deal.

The only indicator that has direct influence on this form of financing is the movement of interest rates up or down, which affects the amount of money circulating in the economy. For that reason, it makes sense to solicit F&F capital during inflationary periods when this market, as well as other potential pools, are more likely to have additional discretionary and/or investment cash available. Make the solicitation during the early stage of inflation, when interest rates are still rising or are about to peak.

PRIVATE INVESTORS

Forms

Exempt Offerings

This financing strategy is the sale of an equity or debt security offered by either a public or a private company, through an underwriter or through a self-underwriting, to a small number of sophisticated or accredited investors for investment rather than resale purposes. A private placement, which also is known as a Regulation D, limited or unregistered offering, is a generic term for all Section 4(6)—or true private placements—and all Regulation D 504, 505, and 506 offerings. These offerings are attractive to business owners and investors because they require only a minimum of filing with the SEC and with state regulatory bodies. In fact, the filing is so simplified that private placements are exempt from some SEC registration requirements under the Securities Act of 1933. (Regulation D of the 1933 Act details the exemptions and the conditions of exemption.)

Hybrid Securities

This is a bond, or senior security, that is exchanged at a later date for a specific number of common shares at a pre-determined price. One example is a convertible debenture. This is a standard debenture or general debt obligation that is subordinated, or junior, and backed solely by the reputation of your company (an unsecured bond). It's an interest-bearing security, so the company must pay investors a set amount of money at intervals as well as the principal amount of the loan at maturity. Any part of the loan principal amount, or all of it, can be convertible into common stock at prices of up to 20 percent higher than market price. Hybrids are issued by small and large companies that need an equity kicker to attract new investors: they provide higher income than common stock, greater appreciation than common bonds, tax benefits for large companies, and more appeal for the offering until greater returns can be achieved.

Example: Lynn Reinner Publishing Co./Boulder, CO

Resource Possibility: Investment banks

Limited Partnership

This is a private or public for-profit business established by one or a small number of general partners and a larger number of limited partners. The partners can be individuals, groups of individuals, or companies. The general partner manages the day-to-day operations of the business for a management fee and a percent of capital gains and/or income in exchange for services and the assumption of debt liability, if any. The limited partners, who are at-risk only for the amount of their investment, finance the business in exchange for capital gains, income, and tax benefits. Private limited partnerships can be sold through a brokerage house to a small number of accredited or sophisticated investors or it can be sold as a self-underwriting. Many limited partnerships are structured to serve specific purposes such as, research and development, income, oil and gas, and master limited partnerships.

Resource Possibility: Investment banks

Warrants (Subscription or Stock-Purchase Warrants)

This security is issued with a bond or preferred stock (common stock is becoming more common) and entitles the shareholder to buy, during a set period of time, a similar ratio of common stock at a specified price set higher than market price at the time of issuance. Warrants are sold primarily to debt investors as an opportunity for equity participation, which increases the marketability of the original fixed-income security. They are transferable and can be traded on the major stock exchanges.

Investor Markets

- Industry associations
- Accounting/legal firm networks
- Venture capital groups/investment clubs
- U.S. and offshore investment/merchant banks
- Commercial banks in the United States
- Large U.S. corporations/insurance companies
- Offshore corporations and government agencies
- Matchmaking database companies
- U.S. and offshore deal-making firms

Offshore Potential

The trend in capital-raising among private investors in the United States is toward more equity dollars chasing fewer and bigger domestic deals. For that reason, many entrepreneurs are taking their exempt offerings to the European and Asian capital markets by way of merchant banks and the private investor networks accessed by international (Big Eight) accounting and legal firms. For the most part, foreign government agencies—through a merchant bank that represents the government as an investor—prefer to be debt lenders, with an option to buy a small percentage of equity participation through warrants.

Also, some small U.S. companies now sell convertible debenture offerings for very small amounts to private offshore corporations. Less willing to be lenders, other private firms and investor networks overseas are willing to invest equity capital in small, higher risk companies in the United States for the opportunity to gain ownership rights, technology transfer rights, higher returns, management/technical skills, or access to a future product line.

Table 3.2
Primary Equity Source Requirements: What Investors Prefer

Source	Revenue	Earnings
Stock market		
Initial public offering	$10 million	10%
ESOP	$250,000 payroll	5%–10%
Warrants	Variable	Increasing
Individuals		
F&F	Variable	Variable
Exempt offerings	$10 million	5%–10%
Corporations		
Joint ventures/ licensing and technology transfer agreements	Variable	High potential
Venture capital	$50 million	30% after-in future tax
Partnerships	Variable	20%+
Merger/buyout	Any size	Increasing
Offshore		
Merchant banks	$5–10 million	20%+
Private market	$5 million+	High potential
Corporations	$5 million+	20%+
Government	Variable by program	Increasing/variable

Table 3.2 *(Continued)*

Source	Growth Potential	Risk
Stock Market		
IPO	Very high	Moderate
ESOP		Low
Warrants	High	Moderate
Individuals		
F&F	N/A	Low
Exempt offerings	Moderate	Moderate
Corporations		
Joint venture/ licensing and technology transfer agreements	High	Moderate
Venture capital	Very high	High
Partnerships	Moderate	Low
Merger/buyout	High	Low
Offshore		
Merchant banks	Moderate	Low
Individuals	Moderate	Moderate
Corporations	High	Moderate
Government	Moderate	Low

Table 3.2 *(Continued)*

Source	Export	Ownership Preference
Stock Market		
IPO	Potential	Majority
ESOP	Variable	Majority
Warrants	Potential	Majority
Individuals		
F&F	Variable	Minority
Exempt offerings	Potential	Minority
Corporations		
Joint ventures/ licensing and technology transfer agreements	Strong potential	Minority
Venture capital	Strong potential	Usually minority
Partnerships	Variable	50%
Merger/buyout	Variable	Majority
Offshore		
Merchant banks	Yes	Minority
Individuals	Yes	Minority
Corporations	Yes	Minority/ownership potential
Government	Potential	Minority

Table 3.2 *(Continued)*

Source	Expected Maturity	Patents
Stock Market		
IPO	Immediate offering	Yes
ESOP	Immediate offering	Yes
Warrants	Months to perpetuity	Yes
Individuals		
F&F	Highly variable	N/A
Exempt offerings	Up to 3 years	Yes
Corporations		
Joint ventures/ licensing and technology transfer agreements	Up to 10 years	Yes
Venture capital	3 to 5 years	Yes
Partnerships	Long-term	Yes
Merger/buyout	Immediate	Yes
Offshore		
Merchant banks	Up to 7 years	Yes
Private market	Up to 3 years	Yes
Corporations	Up to 3 years	Yes
Government	Up to 7 years	Yes

Table 3.2 *(Continued)*

Source	Investor Participation in Your Company	Exit
Stock Market		
IPO	Board seat, voting	Sale
ESOP	Board seat, policy-making, voting	Sale
Warrants	Voting	Sale
Individuals		
F&F	Usually no	Repayment
Exempt offerings	Voting	Sale
Corporations		
Joint ventures/ licensing and technology transfer agreements	No	Profit
Venture capital	Board seat, mgmt. assistance, voting	IPO/Sale
Partnerships	50%	Sale
Merger/buyout	Usually total	Profit
Offshore		
Merchant banks	Board seat, mgmt. assistance	Profit
Individuals	Voting	Profit
Corporations	Mgmt. assistance	Profit
Government		

Table 3.2 *(Continued)*

Source	Niche	Returns
Stock Market		
IPO	Yes	Stock profits
ESOP	N/A	Stock profits
Warrants	Yes	Stock profits
Individuals		
F&F	N/A	Repayment
Exempt offerings	Yes	Cash returns
Corporations		
Joint ventures/ licensing and technology transfer agreements	Yes	Cash returns/ royalties
Venture capital	Yes	30% ann. returns
Partnerships	Variable	Split profits
Merger/buyout	Variable	Higher profits
Offshore		
Merchant banks	Yes	Debt repayment/ cash returns
Individuals	Yes	Cash returns
Corporations	Yes	Cash returns/ royalties
Government	Variable	Debt repayment/ royalties/cash returns

Outside Experts

Brokerage Firms

If you are trying to sell a private offering in the United States, it's a good idea to hire an underwriting firm to find investors when capital for small businesses is scarce. There's a lot of competition for private dollars, so take advantage of all the help you can get selling the offering. If you plan to sell a private offering to off-shore investors, it may not be as important to involve an underwriter: Many offshore offerings are "pre-sold" by the lead source. For example, your international accounting firm may have done most of the selling for you by the time you're put in contact with the offshore investor. If your law firm has international services, it can provide the necessary stock exchange information for both countries.

Accounting Firms

Your financial statements will have to be audited to satisfy investors in your private offering, so hire an accounting firm early on to organize, update, and correct all your financial documentation. Accounting services from inception can save a lot of time and money later when the company is recapitalized. It is imperative to use international accounting firm services if your investors live and work in another country, to adjust currency and foreign exchange calculations, determine applicable tax law in both countries, and file the appropriate documentation for government requirements in both countries.

Law Firms

A law firm should be engaged soon after inception so that corporate documents are reviewed and updated regularly. It will save time-consuming chores such as reorganization of the corporation and complicated legal reviews that must be completed before an offering is sold to public or private investors. If you plan to sell an offering overseas, your law firm should have international services, and specialists in your industry and in small business.

Valuation Professionals

A professional estimation of your company's market value is a very important negotiating point in a private offering, absent publicly held stock that can be compared directly with like companies. A valuation is even more important if the offering is sold to offshore investors who are unfamiliar with the value of similar companies in the United States. Also, the question of eventual technology transfer may arise for later negotiation, when it is even more important to know the value of your company and technology within a global context.

Financial Printers

Government requirements for disclosure and reporting documentation for investors and regulatory bodies make it imperative to use the services of a specialized financial printer with a positive track record in the production of documents you need, such as an offering circular or prospectus, and in your industry, if possible.

Public Relations Firms

If your company operates in a cutting-edge industry, if your target market is bombarded by competitors, or if your product/ technology is so new that no one knows what it is, you probably need to hire the services of a public relations firm to make an impact on your market. Public relations is much more workable if your investors can be reached through media in the United States; it is very difficult to design a public relations program to impress foreign investors unless your potential investors are accessible through specific trade media. Public relations firms will attract media space to describe your product, promote your corporate image, put your management on television and radio talk shows, and plan such promotional events as workshops, charity donations, and community-service projects.

Costs

Brokerage Firms

When IPO activity slows down, the cost of private equity rises in inverse proportion for small business owners. In fact, deals on the small end of the scale cost more as a percent of funds raised than deals on the large end. For the most part, equity financing costs less than a public offering—but not much less. The average brokerage commission for a small financing is 10 percent of the amount raised. Upfront, out-of-pocket, and other expenses designed to take the risk out of the offering can total another 5 to 10 percent of the amount raised.

Attorneys

Although your underwriter will have in-house attorneys to review your documentation, prepare contracts, and file the required compliance material, it is a good idea to have the documentation reviewed by a law firm that represents your company. This expense varies by market, size of financing, and offering complexity; in general, fees for the legal firm total up to 5 percent of the amount raised.

Accountants

If you don't have a CPA or chief financial officer on your management team, hire an outside accounting firm to review the tax and cash flow implications of the financing. This cost is about the same as an outside legal review: 5 percent of the amount raised, contingent on the condition of your financial records.

Valuation Consultants

This variable cost can be negotiated as a flat fee or as a percent of the dollar value of the company. The percent cost ranges from 2 to 8 percent of the established market value.

Financial Printers

If the production of a prospectus or offering circular is required for a stock offering, you will pay $5,000 to $15,000 for printing services.

Public Relations Firms

If you plan to stage successively larger financings in the private or public market at a future date, it's a good idea to start marketing your company name and product well ahead of time. The best way to do that is to hire a firm that specializes in institutional and product advertising and public relations. By the time you're ready to do a large offering, potential investors will have been educated about and sold on your company through the press. These firms charge either by project or by monthly retainer for six months to one year. The average cost by month is $1,000 to $2,000 for basic media services.

Filing

The costs vary according to the nature of the offering, including SEC fees of .02 percent of the maximum aggregate offering price, NASD fees of $100 to $5,100 maximum, transfer agent and registrar fees of $5,000 to $10,000, and varying blue sky fees wherever the offering is sold.

Action Plan to Access the Private Market

One Year Ahead

An offering doesn't take one year to prepare or even sell; but the battle plan for distinguishing your company from all the others trying to raise private equity will take careful planning. Hire the outside experts first because you may need their input very early on, to develop strategies that are effective with divergent groups of investors. The third-party consultation team should include at minimum an attorney and an accountant, an underwriter if applicable who will initiate the planning of your stock offering. All outside consultants and agents should be familiar with your industry and should have a track record in small business financing techniques. Ask for client references. This is also the time to write or rewrite your business plan, to include the most up-to-date financial information, the capital request and the exit strategy for investors. An effective marketing campaign should be launched for those target markets you've identified as key to increased revenues and to potential investments.

Six Months Ahead

At this point, your CPA should prepare historical audited financial statements and highlights of the company's operations as proof of its size and earnings. Include audits of the past three years, and an audited statement of the last fiscal year and quarter. At the same time, your attorney should begin a legal review of all corporate documents, including lease agreements, shareholder or management loans, corporate charter and bylaws, debt outstanding, vendor contracts, stock option or purchase plans, employment contracts and rights of first refusal. If all the outside experts have been brought on board, write a composite list of potentially qualified investors who are likely to conform to the investor limitations mandated by the nature of your offering, such as sophisticated or unaccredited investors.

Three Months Ahead

A placement memorandum or offering circular must be prepared to explain the company and the offering for the benefit of potential investors before they decide to buy in. Governed by S-1 or S-18 requirements of the Securities Act of 1933, this financing memorandum should be prepared with the input of you and your management, your attorney and accountant, and the investment bankers, if applicable. This team also must prepare and produce an investment letter prior to the date on which the sale of the offering can begin. This document, which must be signed by every qualified buyer of private stock, certifies that the signer is buying for investment rather than resale purposes. It also lists the conditions and limitations of the offering. Contingent on the nature of the private offering, you or the underwriter may have to file registration/disclosure documentation with the SEC and/or state regulatory bodies.

Offering Date

Your offering memorandum and investment letter must be available for distribution to potential investors on the date selected for sales to begin. You must also file a notice of sale on Form D within 15 days of the first sale and every six months during sales, as well as a final notice within 30 days after the last sale.

How to Time Private Market Financing

Like all other equity sources, the private market is most generous during periods of rising inflation when interest rates are up, more money is in circulation, private and public company valuations are higher, and the price of nearly everything goes up. Trends in the private market are determined to a large extent by the factors that affect the public market. For small business owners, this means that if the analogous sector of the public market—the new-issues or IPO sector—is suffering or in decline due to certain economic conditions, the private market will suffer too. When this domino affect is in play, private equity will be more expensive, more difficult to attract, and more time-consuming to raise.

Among the economic indicators that affect private equity most directly are global competition and interest rates. The national economy may not be in an acknowledged recession, or even drifting toward it; but your industry, for example, may be experiencing recessionary effects if global competition heats up. When that happens, as it did in the mid-1980s in the semi-conductor industry, there is less capital available for the industry and demand for your product decreases. Most investors prefer to put money into an industry in which there are few or no global competitors because less competition from overseas, from lower priced firms, creates an inflationary effect for your industry: more capital is available and the company can profit from the rising, unmet demand for product.

A boost in interest rate has the same effect on all equity strategies, including private placements and exempt offerings: because it creates an inflationary effect, it is a good time to solicit private investors with an offering in the form of equity or stock. While the rate of interest is still going up, the value and price of your stock presumably will be on the rise also. When interest rates begin to fall significantly, these equity investors tend to avoid equity participations. They will sit out the cycle or look for debt offerings by which to benefit from the downward movement of interest rates.

MERCHANT BANKING

Forms

Merchant Banking/United States

Investment banks in the United States traditionally have acted as agents on behalf of stock-issuing companies that retain them to structure, administer, and sell their corporate stock offerings. Investment banks—brokerage houses or wire houses—sell to both the public and private markets, including private placements, initial and secondary offerings, municipal and corporate bond offerings, and limited partnerships, among many other offerings.

As an agent in a private placement, for example, a brokerage house will structure the offering, administer it, and find outside investors to buy the stock. Typically, the brokerage house does everything but invest in the offering for its own account. That's changing rapidly, however, as more and more investment banks begin to function like merchant banks in Europe and Asia: they put up their own cash, acting as both agent and investor. In many cases, the decision to invest in a deal they have been hired to sell is based on the firm's inability to complete the sale. Rather than lose the financing they've already raised from private investors, the brokerage house will kick in the balance to close out the offering.

There are wide variations in the size of offering a U.S. merchant bank will sell. Most large investment banks won't underwrite an offering under $5 million. They prefer to sell deals in the public market for large corporations and multinationals, worth hundreds of millions of dollars. Regional investment banks prefer high-end deals too, although their minimum size is about $1 million. Thousands of local brokerages, however, are willing to structure private deals in the $500,000 to $1 million range. A few will sell offerings in the $100,000 range; but most offerings this size today are self-underwritings. (See Chapter 5 for more information about the self-underwriting process.)

True merchant banks review a wide range of investment criteria, including deal size and industry niche. They generally prefer to invest in profitable companies that want to recapitalize or that want capital for later-state growth. A typical merchant bank deal in the United States raises from $2 million to $5 million with returns of about 20 percent annually over a three- to five-year period. If the merchant bank invests early, it helps sales to outside investors. In exchange, merchant bankers often want to be the lead investor, or have representation on your board of directors for tighter control over your operating budget.

Merchant Banking/Offshore

Offshore merchant banks operate somewhat differently. Like merchant banks in the United States, they also act as both agent and investor. But because offshore merchant banks often represent their government's financing policies as an agency of the government, they seek greater control over the capital they invest in your company and may require more disclosure. They do more due diligence on you and your company. Their screening process is more stringent, particularly in requirements for the analysis of global trading conditions, offshore environmental effects, and local employment/tax impact. To offset the severity of these requirements, offshore merchant banks offer management counseling and project development services that can far surpass the services offered by their U.S. counterparts. Offshore merchant banks tend to specialize by industry and by the needs of their local economy. Many finance only high-tech companies that are promise big returns in three to five years; others finance companies that have technologies they can import to the local economy to stimulate employment, local manufacturing, and future product lines.

Investor Markets

- Commercial banks/U.S.
- Investment banks/U.S.
- Private merchant banks/U.S. and offshore

Costs

Interest (Offshore)

The primary cost of merchant banking is interest expense during the life of the loan. If you are not a strong negotiator, it may be worthwhile to use your legal counsel or another adviser as your representative when the terms of the contract are set.

Brokerage Firms (U.S.)

In the United States, many so-called merchant banks charge an underwriter's commission of 7 to 10 percent, usually closer to 10 percent, to close your deal by buying up the unsold portion of the offering. Underwriters may require that you pay upfront, nonaccountable expenses of 2.5 to 5 percent of the net proceeds.

Attorneys

Although your merchant/investment bank will have in-house attorneys to review your documentation, prepare contracts, and file the required compliance material, it's a good idea to hire your own law firm to represent your interests in the deal. This expense varies by local market conditions, size of financing, and complications that arise from doing business overseas, if applicable. In general, fees for the legal firm total up to 10 percent of the amount raised.

Accountants

The company also should retain an accounting firm that represents your interests and works with the merchant bank's financial staff. This cost is about the same as outside legal representation: 10 percent of the amount raised, contingent on the condition of your financial records and the complexity of the financing.

Liaison/Consulting Firms

If the merchant bank is offshore, you may incur consulting expenses for such things as negotiations in a foreign language, cultural consulting, or pre-travel services. The cost of retaining a liaison firm can range from $1,000 to $10,000, depending on the extent of its services.

Action Plan to Access Offshore Merchant Banks

One Year Ahead

Hire an accountant and attorney to audit the company's financial statements, and review all contracts and documentation. Be sure the accountant performs a tax analysis on the company's operations in order to assess the financial and tax impact of doing business with an offshore entity.

Ten Months Ahead

Begin to identify, locate and pre-screen merchant bank candidates in other countries, using a third-party as liaison, a consulting firm that specializes in matching companies with capital sources, or a list of referrals you've gathered from networking international business groups.

Eight Months Ahead

After you've selected two or three merchant banks as potential matches, request their loan application criteria in writing and a loan application. Prepare the loan application and adapt your business plan to include the effects of operations in offshore markets. The attorney and accountant should guide the preparation and execution of these materials. (See Chapter 2 for information about what should be included in a financing request to an offshore entity.)

Six Months Ahead

Submit your loan application with a cover letter and adapted business plan. Contact the merchant banks in one month to follow up your request and offer to provide other documentation, as needed.

How to Time Merchant Bank Financing

Merchant banks in offshore markets and investment firms in the United States that function like merchant banks are technically attuned to economic indicators that affect both the public and the private market. Most larger firms have strategic planners and/or economists who study the movement of prime, interest, and mortgage rates; the movement of key currencies around the world; and the flow of investment cash among relevant trading nations. You will be more successful at getting cash from merchant banks if you understand the level of economic sophistication and sensitivity at which they operate. Sell a financing package that emphasizes equity when the U.S. economy and your industry's health are inflationary or when interest rates are going up; solicit loan/stock financing during a recessionary period or as interest rates fall to catch bond rates on the way up.

When a merchant bank is located offshore, there are secondary factors to consider. If the foreign country is in recession, there will be less cash available to invest in you regardless of the merit of your company or product. In contrast, foreign inflation helps your cause, contingent on how well your product or technology fills a local need and enhances the local economy. If global competitors have saturated that country, the recessionary impact of less available cash—it is chasing exports from other countries—could diminish or eliminate any possibility of financing in that country. Another foreign influence is the local stock market: what does the public market in that country favor in terms of industries, technologies, and emerging products? How does the local stock market react to a sudden outbreak of war in another part of the globe?

STRATEGIC ALLIANCES

Corporate Partnering (Strategic Alliances)

A contracted relationship between a small, start-up company with a proprietary or unique product, service, or technology and a larger corporation with the resources, expertise, financing, distribution network, and/or salesforce to help develop, commercialize, and/or sell the product.

Technology Transfer

The transfer of ownership of a proprietary, patent-protected technology through technology transfer agreements, joint ventures, and other contracts, from one individual, company, or government to another. The technology transfer trend is reaching significant levels between small, U.S. technology-based firms and overseas investors who represent buyers for both developed and Third World nations. Another growing trend is the reverse flow of technology: former net importers of technology, such as Japan, now export technology to Western nations.

Corporate Culture

The synergy of management's distinctive style, the employee mindset, and the company's mission statement, and its affect on operations, corporate image, and growth potential; the general milieu created by a combination of forces within the company: the company is paternalistic, with on-site daycare centers and management-sponsored carpools for all employees; or a company is egalitarian, with a bottom-up as well as a top-down decision-making process, and a relaxed dress code for all employees.

Divorce Settlement

The exit strategy and compensation plan for both parties to a strategic alliance; a method for dividing up the assets, liabilities, trade secrets, and personnel in a joint business or project when one or both partners wants to terminate the agreement. The divorce settlement, or termination clauses, in a strategic alliance partnership can comprise up to 80 percent of the content in a typical joint-venture agreement.

Risk Sharing

This concept is growing in importance to both large equity investors and to the small business owners they finance. It is an analytical and conscious process of identifying and allocating risks more evenly between the investor and the entrepreneur/company. When the capital markets are leery of financing startup companies because of a perceived increase in risk due to such economic factors as rising interest rates or a dollar decline in the initial public offering market, private equity investors often try to pass some of the risk to the entrepreneur, especially in small, private stock offerings. As interest rates continue to rise, strategic alliance partners who foot the bill are beginning to follow the same trend.

Horizontal Joint Venture

A business entity or project between two partners which competes in the same industries as both parties to the agreement. A vertical joint venture indicates activity that flows to other industries upstream and downstream from the joint venture's industry, such as a user of packaging, warehousing, process innovation, or other outside services.

Forms

Corporate Partnering

A partnership agreement between a start-up firm and a large corporation in the same or a related industry is actually a rarity among the available forms of corporate partnering. More often, the term is used loosely to denote one of the following forms of strategic alliance.

Licensing Agreement

This is a strategy, usually between like entities, for example, two individuals or two companies, by which one company sells certain rights to another company to market/sell, manufacture or distribute its product, service, or technology. A typical licensing agreement allows a small, high-tech company that needs financing to complete product development and sales/distribution help when the product is commercialized to sell rights to a larger company in the same industry, which has a compatible product line and an existing sales/distribution pipeline. The income potential for both the licensor and licensee is determined by the development stage of the product, and the nature of the legal rights that protect the product, such as patent, trademark, or copyright.

Technology Transfer Agreement

A technology transfer agreement is very similar to a licensing arrangement. However, the transfer of ownership rights to the technology in this agreement applies more often to offshore licensees who want to buy all rights to the technology. For that reason, technology transfer agreements are more complex transactions in which legal implications, technical data, protection clauses, nonperformance, and global issues are covered much more thoroughly.

Joint Venture

This is a relationship between two or more parties who agree to create a project or structure a corporate entity that is operated and controlled by the investors. A joint venture can be formed as a corporation, partnership or undivided interest to research, develop, manufacture, distribute or sell a product. In the small business sector, a small firm contracts with a larger company in the same industry to produce or sell a compatible product or technology. The large company gets an equity stake in your business; you get the financing and resources needed to develop and commercialize the product. A joint venture also is called, sometimes mistakenly, a research and development agreement, a joint venture marketing agreement, a manufacturing or distribution agreement, or a collaborative agreement.

Research and Development Agreement

This structure typically is a limited partnership between a small company with a development-stage product or technology and a group of investors who function like shareholders in a corporation. The general partner, responsible for the day-to-day research and development function, is the sponsoring small business; the limited partners are the investors, who finance the project in exchange for royalties of between 25 and 45 percent and a tax-benefit package. The general partner is paid, after a certain performance period, on a fixed-fee or cost-plus basis. An R&D partnership, which can be sold to private or public investors, is a flexible instrument that can raise from $50,000 for a start-up firm to over $50 million for a large corporation.

Marketing/Manufacturing Agreement

Typically, the transfer of marketing or manufacturing ownership rights to a product or technology is transacted with a licensing, technology transfer, or joint venture agreement that is specified for this purpose.

Limited Partnerships

Most limited partnerships not formed around a research and development project raise at least $250,000 for the general partner. The complexities and related expenses of the limited partnership structure make it unsuitable in most cases for a financing of $100,000 or less, although there have been a few exceptions. This partnership is established between one or a small number of general partners who manage the day-to-day activities of the project and the limited partners who finance it. This is an extremely flexible structure for investors, in contrast to a corporation for example, and offers tax benefits as well as investment returns to the limited partners. The general partner is paid a management fee and a percent of capital gains and/or income as compensation for managing the project and assuming debt liability, if applicable.

Investor Markets

- Large corporations
- Competitors/vendors
- Universities
- Incubators
- Foreign governments/corporations
- Small Business Investment Research program/U.S. government

Offshore Potential

Because the limited partnership has been a tax-driven financing vehicle, the deductions and benefits that result from either a profit or a loss on the project are not of use to most offshore investors unless they file a U.S. tax return.

Costs

Accounting Firms

An analysis of the tax and cash flow results of your strategic alliance will cost between $3,000 and $10,000 for a transaction in the $100,000 range, depending on the condition of your company's financial records, the domicile of your alliance partner, and the complexity of the alliance structure. If your alliance partner is a foreign corporation, the accounting cost can be 10 to 20 percent higher.

Attorneys

Most law firms charge entrepreneurial clients about 5 percent of the amount financed through the strategic alliance for the preparation of legal documents, contract negotiation, and/or a corporate review of all documents.

Deal-Brokers

The intermediary who finds a domestic strategic alliance partner for the company also may provide other services for the transaction, including accounting, legal, valuation, or other functions that increase the finder's fee. Depending on the nature of the services provided, a deal-broker charges from 2 to 8 percent of the amount financed through the transaction.

Liaison/Consulting Firms (Offshore Partner)

The intermediary who finds an offshore strategic alliance partner for the company usually charges more than a deal-broker who matches two domestic companies. In exchange for cultural consulting, accounting and tax advice related to the foreign country, advice on foreign negotiating styles, and other services, the firm that specializes in foreign agreements charges from 5 to 10 percent of the amount financed in the agreement.

Action Plan to Access Strategic Alliance Financing

Six Months Ahead

A market study should be commissioned, preferably from a professional marketing research firm that specializes in your industry, to measure the profit potential of your product or technology. (See Chapter 2 for the specific inclusions recommended in the Market Analysis section.)

When the results of the market study are compiled, a business plan should be written incorporating the market study results, an extensive analysis of a proposed strategic alliance project, a separate feasibility analysis of the technology or product, and a manufacturing plan for the alliance project—as well as the standard business plan inclusions.

Begin to identify, locate, and pre-screen potential strategic alliance partners based on industry compatibility, product/technology compatibility, or complementary strengths and weaknesses. Develop your own list of candidates and solicit references and leads from people you know and trust.

If you plan to structure a joint venture agreement, incorporate the company in order to simplify the agreement and to assign project responsibilities more easily to specific corporate entities participating in the agreement.

Five Months Ahead

Develop a list of negotiation points for the strategic alliance contract, including such factors as the amount financed, the terms, the exit strategy you prefer, the divorce settlement when the alliance disbands for any reason, nonperformance issues, patent or copyright protection, ownership rights, valuation method preferred, trade secrets, distribution of tax credits or other benefits, and the potential for an on-going relationship with your alliance partner.

Four Months Ahead

Hire an accounting firm to review your financial records and provide audited statements for review by your strategic alliance partner. Your CPA also should project the tax and cash flow results of a potential strategic alliance.

One Month Ahead

When a strategic alliance partner has been identified in principle, hire an attorney or law firm that specializes in small business and in your industry to prepare the necessary contract documentation. The same attorney may be willing to negotiate the contract for you, if you prefer. If the strategic alliance is a joint venture with a large, public corporation, your attorney should review certain documentation that must be filed by your partner's attorney with the SEC, and with state regulatory agencies to comply with federal and state reporting/disclosure requirements.

How to Time Strategic Alliance Financing

A majority of strategic alliances are formed to fulfill short-term corporate missions for both parties in the deal, such as to develop a specific technology, to distribute one product, or to penetrate one market for a period of time. This trend suggests two things:

1. Large or offshore companies are willing to do strategic alliances under almost any economic conditions because they have a specific, dedicated purpose and they can exit the deal easily if economic conditions deteriorate badly.

2. The only economic indicator that has a direct influence on strategic alliance financing is interest rates, which encourage or discourage the amount of cash available for investments through the number and depth of inflationary effects.

If you need equity financing from a strategic alliance, solicit funding during a rising inflationary trend. If interest rates start to decline and recessionary effects are in play, emphasize cash less and corporate resources more. Ask for less capital in exchange for lab space, management assistance, technical support, facilities, equipment, or whatever you need to commercialize and sell your product.

If you want debt financing in the form of a loan and/or a line of credit, for example, look for a strategic alliance when interest rates are falling and other recessionary signals are in play. If interest rates stay high and you still want a loan, ask for a smaller loan plus additional corporate resources from your strategic alliance partner.

Global competition is an economic indicator of secondary importance when you look for a strategic alliance, unless the competition is focused on your industry. If your industry is glutted with competitors, it will be difficult to form an effective strategic alliance unless you have an impeccable strategy for taking market share. A high level of global competition creates a recession for the industry when U.S. capital flows toward the foreign manufacturer instead of back into the U.S. economy where it becomes part of the national investment pool. The most successful alliances are formed with a larger company in order to preempt the entry of U.S. or foreign competitors, or before the market is dominated by any one company. This creates an inflationary effect in which capital stays in the industry and in the United States as reinvestment or development funding.

PUBLIC MARKET

Forms

Initial Public Offering (IPO)

The public market for shares of assetless, low-cost, or start-up companies trying to go public has diminished significantly since the stock market crash in October 1987. In fact, the IPO market has not yet revived completely. For the first six months of 1988, only 132 U.S. companies sold new issues to raise $12.8 billion. For the same period in 1987, 317 companies went public to raise $14.9 billion. This says two things to business owners and investors who hope to cash out of their investments through the IPO market in the future:

1. The number of companies going public has declined a drastic 66 percent since 1987.

2. The new issues that become successful stock offerings represent companies that can command much larger amounts of capital from investors.

This means if you want to take the company public, it will be judged the old-fashioned way on such fundamental values as revenue history, earnings, and assets. The steak will count more than the sizzle, no matter how good your story is. Public investors will look for projections that are realistic for the current economic environment.

Reliance on public financing can be more dangerous than ever for the small, nontechnology company. You will labor under the investor perception that only strong performers in high-growth sectors can weather any softening in the equity market. And nontech companies only recently have been welcomed in the IPO market. Before 1987, high-tech and speculative companies seemed to be the only IPO candidates able to raise capital with high enough valuations to surpass what private individual and institutional investors completed in their last rounds of financing. There are other dangers. Many investment banks transformed the financial industry with massive consolidations which have resulted in the creation of a reduced number of New York City-based underwriting firms that no longer can afford to take smaller firms public. These "wire-houses" and institutional wholesalers try to increase the offering minimum to a profitable level at the expense of small companies that don't qualify for the offering minimum. As a result, there are too few quality underwriting firms that support small issues for nontechnology companies.

Another danger is the trend in price/earnings multiples, which depend on the conditions in your industry and your company's stock market valuation. Growth industries establish higher multiples because they are bigger and grow faster. Also, your company performance relative to competitors becomes a strong determining factor in the level of multiple used as an industry standard, as well as an emerging trend in the industry or market. Your future acquisition strategy has an effect on a potential IPO. High-tech companies will probably generate more internal growth than smaller companies in both the manufacturing and service sectors. But you can leapfrog their internal growth rate through the acquisition of complementary or niche companies and end up comparatively ahead.

One of the most serious problems associated with an IPO is the frequent inability of management and investors to sell stock. Only in the most bullish markets do underwriters allow seller participation in the sale, which usually doesn't exceed 25 percent of the offering from insider selling. Once your company is publicly held, the stock is considered subject to holding periods, 144 volume limitations, and the effect on management of large institutional purchases of stock.

If capital has been raised in the public market to transact a leveraged buyout with outside investors, the offering proceeds are used solely for debt repayment. As owner, that means only the outright sale of the company will create liquidity for you.

Blind Pool (Shell)

This is a limited partnership that doesn't specify to public or private investors (the limited partners) the companies or properties to be acquired by the general partner. Many small, private companies with strong cash flow or salable assets are merged by a blind pool into a larger, cashless public company in order to short-cut some of the costs and time involved in going public. Blind pools have been regulated more scrupulously since the mid-1980s after the quality of many blind-pool deals had deteriorated dangerously and unprofitably for unwary retail investors.

(Public) Limited Partnership

This is a for-profit business entity comprised of a small number of, or one, general partner who manages the project day-to-day and a larger number of limited partners who finance it. Shares in a public limited partnership can be bought by any number of investors starting at about $5,000 per unit of stock in the partnership. (Private limited partnerships can be sold to a maximum of 35 unaccredited investors and to an unlimited number of accredited, or sophisticated, investors who buy in for $50,000 per unit or more.) Certain partnerships are structured for service organizations, including income partnerships, oil and gas partnerships, master limited partnerships (nearly extinct due to recent tax reform), and research and development partnerships. In the early 1980s, changes in tax and regulatory requirements made compliance and the sale of limited partnerships more difficult for companies of every virtually every size. Limited partnership offerings generally raise a minimum of $200,000, although some partnerships are created to raise as little as $100,000 through the sale of stock.

Employee Stock Option Plan (ESOP)

The employee investor market may become an increasingly popular option for companies that have languished in the absence of a strong public market for startup stocks. An Employee Stock Ownership Plan (ESOP) is a trust that sells corporate shares to employees of the company at no cost instead of to the public market. Employees then have a vested interest in the performance of the company and its shares, which increases productivity and protects the company against hostile suitors.

Convertible Debenture/Debt

Small, high-risk companies frequently have to offer an equity deal sweetener to lure debt investors. The lure is a convertible feature in the corporate security, usually preferred stock or bonds, which can be exchanged for a preset number of common shares or another form of security at a preset price.

Investor Markets

High-Risk Investors, Retail or Mutual Fund

These are the investors who comprised the majority of the penny stock market in the early 1980s, and still hunt for bargains among the few low-priced stocks that come public every year. Typically, they are willing to take more risks for fewer dollars with a concept-stage or seed company than most middle-of-the-road retail or blue-chip investors. They buy shares individually through a brokerage house or collectively through a mutual fund. If you're determined to sell stock in the public market, find these investors through penny stock or over-the-counter (OTC) publications and newsletters, through local investment clubs, and through entrepreneurial and venture capital associations or clubs.

Lenders/Debt Investors

Your solicitation will not appeal to the public market as straight debt, which usually starts at the $20 million level. But a small, high-risk deal can be sold more easily with the promise of an equity kicker or deal sweetener in the form of common shares. The convertible security, which is usually preferred stock or a bond, is exchanged at a later date at a preset price. If your company prospects are exciting but the venture is high-risk, cash flow has been nonexistent, or asset value has not increased appreciably, a convertible security may be the only offering to sell to debt investors/lenders.

Employees

This market invests very selectively as a group of employees in order to own and/or control the company for which they work. This is a relatively untapped market of investors, although the number of U.S. companies that have adopted ESOP or similar ownership plans has increased steadily since 1974. Today, about 9 million Americans in roughly 9,000 companies are protected by ESOP programs. ESOPs offer five advantages over other forms of corporate ownership. They create an easy way to:

1. Buy you out when you want to retire

2. Structure additional employee benefits

3. Borrow money

4. Start a new business

5. Prevent hostile takeovers.

Geographical Market

With the passage of blue-sky laws in several states during the 1980s, volume activity shows less volatility among local markets. However, some states still show higher levels of lower-priced stock activity, including Utah, which was the unofficial blind pool capital of the United States for most of the 1980s, and Colorado, which was the (OTC) capital during the late 1970s and early 1980s.

Shell Company Management

Occasionally, investors who avoid the small-issues market can be enticed to buy an offering that combines a cash-poor public company (a shell company) and a private company with lots of assets or cash flow. Combined, these companies offer investors in the public market new opportunities for profit that, presumably, didn't exist for either company separately. (For more information on blind pools, see Chapter 5.)

Offshore Potential

If investors believe the company has strong fundamentals, or a lock on a new industry or technology, the opportunity for offshore market penetration resulting from a sale of shares to the public market is good. The opportunity could come from two sources:

1. From the proceeds of the sale of shares, which could cover the cost of marketing and distributing to end-users overseas

2. From the networking and contacts of the other party to the sale of shares, including corporations as limited partners in a limited partnership and the shell company in a blind-pool deal.

Third-Party Professionals

Lenders/Consultants

If you use a lender as a third-party professional to develop or groom your convertible security offering to other debt investors, make sure this professional can answer these questions: Is your deal too small by today's market standards? Can you change the deal at the last minute? Will you be buried in paperwork and excessive disclosure reporting? What kind of rate can you negotiate? Find a lender/consultant who is willing to work with you throughout the entire offering process, learns enough about your business to teach you something about it, and is highly regarded by clients or customers.

Professional Valuators

Before the financing package is prepared, you establish a professional valuation of the company's market value so that you're in a better negotiating stance with equity investors. The valuation firm is usually a consulting practice that offers its services by industry specialty. The valuator should provide client references from similar companies in the small-business sector.

Resource Possibility: MB Valuation Services, Inc./Dallas, TX

Underwriters

The underwriter, as the intermediary between your company and public investors in a stock offering, will plan, manage, sell, and support the offering, as well as counsel management before, during, and after the offering. The underwriter usually is an investment banking firm, which should have a track record in small

IPOs and in your industry. (See Chapter 5 for information about self-underwritings.)

Law Firms

Most small companies need help before a stock offering to reorganize the corporate structure and to conduct an all-out legal review of existing documentation, including contracts or agreements on shareholder or management loans, corporate charter and bylaws, stock option or purchase plans, rights of first refusal, and vendor relationships. The law firm also works with the underwriting team and its in-house attorneys to prepare the appropriate documentation for regulatory compliance related to the offering.

Accounting Firms

The accounting firm should be hired well before the offering is planned in order to get the company's financial records updated and audited. The public sale of stock is governed by many tax and regulatory requirements regarding the accuracy of financial records and your responsibility to disclose financial information to investors and to the government. The accounting firm will insure that these financial records are accurate, updated, disclosed to the government, and accessible by investors.

Financial Printers

This highly specialized vendor produces all the documentation required for required shareholder communication and for compliance with government disclosure and reporting requirements regarding the sale of your stock, including the prospectus, offering circular (placement memorandum), quarterly and annual reports to the shareholders, and meeting notices, among others. Because these documents must be completely accurate and produced within a narrow timeframe to conform to industry production standards, your financial printer should be experienced in securities documentation and should have a track record for producing the documents you need. The printer's operating schedule should be managed efficiently and priced fairly within the market.

Public Relations Firms

If your company stock will be sold to the public markets, and to some extent to private markets, it may be good business practice to investigate the use of public relations services to maintain your corporate image in the marketplace after the quiet period is over. This is a specialized corporate function which should be delegated to outside consultants who are experts in media and investor communication. These firms work on a project, monthly-retainer or percentage basis to maintain positive contact with print and broadcast media, plan seminars and workshops, conduct market research, and/or conduct special events and exhibitions. Ask public relations firm candidates for references from small-business clients in your industry to screen their track record. Determine how often stories were planted with the media, how often the company was mentioned in general coverage, or how often company management was sought as "experts" for broadcast programming or public appearances.

Resource Possibility: Pratt and Peifer/San Francisco, CA

Costs

Underwriter Commissions

By NASD regulation, this fee cannot exceed 10 percent of the proceeds of the stock offering. Small offerings, under $1 million, are almost always charged the full 10 percent; as the deal gets larger, this commission is reduced as a percentage of the proceeds.

Broker Fees and Reimbursements

Many brokerage houses charge the company in advance for their legal and other fees, and for nonaccountable expenses. This is in addition to a minimum fee of 2.5 percent of the value of the offering for early nonaccountable expenses.

Attorneys

Legal fees can vary widely, contingent on the accuracy of your corporate records, the amount of reorganization required to clean up your corporate structure, and other "environmental" factors. You will spend about 10 percent of the net proceeds on legal fees.

Accountants

Accounting firm fees are generally about the same amount as legal fees, about 10 percent of the net proceeds, because auditing and other pre-offering services require about the same level of participation.

Filing

SEC filing costs .02 percent of the maximum aggregate offering price. NASD filing costs $100 plus .01 percent of the maximum aggregate offering price, up to $5,100 maximum. Blue sky filing can range up to $15,000 per state. Registrar and transfer agent fees fall between $5,000 and $10,000 per offering.

Documentation

Financial printing for a small offering costs between $10,000 and $20,000 for the prospectus and other preliminary documentation. This cost ranges from $5,000 to $50,000 if color photographs are used.

Public Relations

A public relations firm, working by project or by monthly retainer, usually charges between $1,000 and $2,000 per month for standard media contact and shareholder relations services.

Action Plan to Access Public Financing

Two Years Ahead

Approximately two years before the effective date of the stock offering, you should be initiating four activities:

1. Develop and write a business plan that also acts as a financial package, with complete enough information for potential investors, underwriters, and the media.

2. Develop and begin to execute a corporate image/marketing campaign that pre-sells target investors long before the offering date.

3. Reorganize the company's legal structure from joint venture or partnership to incorporation, recapitalizing and/or splitting the stock forward or backward to adjust the pricing level at which the offering will be sold.

4. Hire a legal firm to conduct a review of all corporate documents, agreements, and contracts.

One Year Ahead

Two long-range personnel issues should be decided:

1. Key management vacancies should be filled, including chief financial officer and other functions most often substituted by small business owners to reduce salary overhead.

2. Outside experts and technical support professionals should be identified, pre-screened, interviewed, and hired. When the underwriting firm is hired, begin early to negotiate the terms of the underwriter contract: commission/discount, stock options, warrants, nonaccountable expenses, and others. Also negotiate the letter of intent, type of underwriting, offering price and size, and right of first refusal on future offerings.

Six Months Ahead

A planning session should be arranged for company management, attorneys and accountants, and the underwriter team of brokers and in-house attorneys. The agenda includes the terms of the offering, the type of offering to be sold, and the delegation of specific offering responsibilities for the preparation of Parts I and II of the registration statement, by time/flow chart.

Three Months Ahead

After the registration statement is filed with the SEC, a "road show" for the prospective broker syndicate is planned using a "red herring" or preliminary prospectus to describe the company and the offering. During the same period, the SEC evaluates the registration statement and determines the revisions you will have to make before an effective date for the offering can be set. The prospectus must be submitted to the NASD, which approves it for compliance to fairness practices regarding underwriter compensation. Up to 90 days after the effective date, management and the underwriters must refrain from disclosing information about the company that is not found in the prospectus or its amendments. During the quiet period, the offering is blue-skied to satisfy state securities regulations where the offering will be sold. Then a due diligence meeting is called for all offering participants during which final questions about the company or the offering are raised. The night before or the morning of the effective date, the offering price, underwriter's commission, and net proceeds are determined. This data, plus any revisions to the registration statement, are filed as the pricing amendment.

How to Time Public Market Financing

If you seek equity or debt financing from the stock market, it will be imperative to consider all primary economic indicators to understand what the market reacts to. Leading stock market indices like the Dow Jones Industrial Average are sensitive barometers that measure most closely the impact of such news headlines as war, acts of terrorism, a change in monetary policy in the United States or abroad, the U.S. imbalance of trade and global competition, and many other secondary factors. Although your $100,000 financing is at the bottom of the low range of offerings in the market, you can maximize your offering by timing it to the events that impact mega-sized companies on the New York or American Stock Exchange.

The stock market flourishes under inflationary trends and retreats under recession. Any events that raise interest rates, keep offshore competitors at home, prevent war-like aggression in any part of the world, and keep the dollar cheap relative to key world currencies is potentially inflationary, or good, for the market. Those trends usually mean that the price of stock goes up for most industries, and that the underlying corporations are valuated higher than in plateau or recessionary periods (Table 3.3).

Table 3.3
Cost Comparison of Domestic and Offshore Equity Sources

Source	Domestic	Offshore
Public investors		
IPO	40%	40%
Warrants	25%	25%
Private investors		
Exempt offerings	35%	40%
F&F	$1–2,000	N/A
Corporations		
Joint venture/licensing and technology transfer agreements	15%	30%
Venture capital	30–49% equity	Highly variable
Merger/buyout	10%	15%

MERGERS/BUYOUTS

The sale of your company, in part or as a whole entity, can be an effective way to raise capital for just about anything you want to finance. Many entrepreneurs use the capital to start up another company, or to fund retirement from the corporate world. Or you can just take the money and run. The key to a profitable sale is making earnings. If your company makes money, it will be in demand by a sometimes surprising variety of potential buyers. After that, your success depends on knowing the kind of deals that are possible in your market and industry, and knowing what you want out of the sale.

Forms

Straight Cash

Most cash sales are based on a multiple of aftertax earnings by industry, usually five to ten times earnings. Your price should approximate the company's current book value, which should be established prior to the transaction by a valuation expert for your industry and market. Most buyers look for a return of at least 25 percent on their investment in your company. For a cash sale, you may have to set a slightly lower selling price and pay a capital gains tax in the year of the sale. But you get out free and clear. The best cash offers tend to come from larger companies and from bidders who shop early to get the best deals. Be prepared for bidders who want to pay only for what's in the company today—not for the company's earnings potential. W.T. Grimm & Co. in Chicago, which tracks merger activity nationwide, reported that 55 percent of all mergers in the first half of 1988 were for cash, up from 40 percent in 1987 when the booming stock market gave companies the ability to finance these transactions more easily by offering equity.

Leveraged Buyout (LBO)

The leverage buyer uses your company's assets as the collateral for a bank loan to pay you off. Because you may have to wait for the money, an LBO sale price can be somewhat higher than a sale or merger price. You should get cash upfront, and notes secured by company stock, which is payable in installments over a certain period of time. When this technique is used by small firms, about 85 percent of the price is leveraged on accounts receivable, 40 to 60 percent on inventory. The payout period is usually five to seven years, based on an interest rate that is pegged two or three percentage points above prime rate. If the company has enough assets to support bank loans but is low on earnings, or if the potential buyers think they can trim operating margins to increase earnings, a small leveraged buyout works very effectively. Called "sons of leveraged buyouts" in the small business sector, LBOs are used more frequently than straight cash sales because it rewards both parties: there is room to sweeten the deal for the seller and the buyer gets a break on upfront costs.

In the last few years, there has been a pervasive change in commercial asset-based lending, from a conventional, formularized strategy in some form to a strategy based on cash flow and business values. The new approach is called "business value lending (BVL)," which signifies that your company's value totals more than individual asset values added together. Value should be viewed as the amount of money that would be paid by a sophisticated investor for the rights to projected future cash flows. When market activity created a demand for non-traditional financing structures, market-driven lenders in this industry segment began to provide BVL to owners who wanted to cash in on increasing LBO activity as well as on the higher prices paid as a multiple of the company's cash flow. Higher prices tend to generate a demand for additional debt, relative to the liquidation values of your assets, which might not have increased. When the company's credit is strong, this financing is easy to get. Lenders like it because BVL is measured through a discounted future cash flow formula or a market multiple comparison that is the lender's second line of defense if cash flow doesn't cover the loan payments. The risk is the necessity to sell the business or its product lines as opposed to the forced liquidation of collateral. Business value lenders that service the small-business market are found through asset-based lending firms. Most large asset-based lenders won't make loans of less than $1 million to $5 million because profits on the loan are considered too low. But local and regional ABLs, especially independent firms, or the BVL department of a commercial bank, often will accommodate this market.

Resources Possibility: Capital Funding Group, Security Pacific Business

Credit, Inc./San Diego, CA

Celtic Capital Corp./Los Angeles, CA

Earnout

This is a variation of the cash sale that is used when you are more optimistic about the company's prospects than the potential buyer is. You agree to accept a lower selling price and continue running the company during an "earnout period" that can last up to five years. In exchange, you get a salary and a percentage of the profits above a negotiated level. The risk to you, of course, is that the company won't perform as well as you thought it would. And while you retain control of the profits, the new owners are in control of the books.

Stock Swaps

A tax-free exchange of stock usually will net more than either cash, or cash and notes; but this technique puts you at-risk for the buyer's stock. If the buyer's stock trades publicly at 10 to 12 times earnings or more, you get more money and no current capital-gains tax liability. The buyer "pays" in high-priced stock instead of in cash, incurs no liabilities, and improves his company's price-earnings ratio through the deal. A stock swap is used when you think the buyer's company is less risky than yours. Most buyers will try to make a swap for assets first, rather than for stock, so they can depreciate the assets quickly.

Table 3.4
Cost Comparison of Primary Debt Sources

Source	Commission	Legal
Stock market		
Convertibles	7–10% + exps	5%
Individuals		
F&F	0	Minimal
Private market	7–10% + exps	5–10%
Lending institutions		
Banks	0; 1–5% if dealbroker used	Minimal
State/fed. govt.	0	Minimal
LBOs	0	$2–5,000
Corporations		
Pooled comm'l paper	0	$2–5,000
Insurance companies	0	$2–5,000
Offshore		
Merchant banks	Variable	10–20%
Individuals	10% + exps	10–20%
Corporations	Variable	10–20%

Table 3.4 *(Continued)*

Source	Accounting	Financial Printer
Stock market		
Convertibles	5%	$5–15,000
Individuals		
F&F	$1–2,000	0
Private market	5–10%	$5–15,000
Lending institutions		
Banks	Minimal	0
State/Fed. govt.	$1–2,000	0
LBOs	$1–2,000	0 unless 1 firm is public
Corporations		
Pooled comm'l paper	1–2,000	0
Insurance co's	5–10%	0
Offshore		
Merchant banks	10–20%	0
Private market	10–20%	$15–20,000
Corporations	10–20%	0
Government	Minimal	0

Investor Markets

- Competitors
- Past and current employees
- Vendors
- Sales representatives
- Larger, compatible corporations
- Clients/customers

Table 3.5
Primary Debt Source Requirements: What Lenders Prefer

Source	Revenue	Earnings
Stock market		
Convertible	$10 million	5–10%
Lending institutions		
LBOs	$5 million	Industry multiple
Banks	$1 million	Industry multiple
Offshore		
Merchant banks	$5 million US	20%
Private market	$5 million US	10%+
Corporations	$5 million US	Industry multiple
Government	Variable	Industry multiple

- Friends and family (F&F)
- Foreign representatives of investor groups, merchant banks, and corporations
- Previously interested parties

Offshore Potential

According to W.T. Grimm & Company statistics, more U.S. businesses are being sold to offshore buyers than ever before. One reason is the weakness of the dollar in comparison to other currencies. Another reason: many foreign purchasers are willing to pay top dollar, unlike their American counterparts, for the products and technologies they can't get in their own countries. Instead of developing the products or technologies they need from the ground up—and often handicapped by the lack of appropriate technology base—they've discovered it's cheaper to buy U.S. knowledge, patents or manufacturing/marketing rights outright.

For this reason, the owner of a high-tech business in the United States currently has the best opportunity to make from 10 to 50 percent more profit by selling his company to a foreign, rather than a U.S., buyer.

There are several ways to access foreign buyers: by networking through Big Eight accounting firms and legal firms that have international offices, by participating in offshore trade missions and exhibitions sponsored by the U.S. Department of Commerce, by registering your products with various federal government agencies that distribute product lists overseas, by hiring a U.S.-based international matchmaking firm that brings buyers and sellers together, and by attracting offshore buyers through articles and advertising in trade publications and business media.

Outside Experts

Some of the best leads for buyers can come from the third-party professionals you hire to help you complete a merger/buyout: accountants, attorneys, deal-brokers, merger/acquisition (M/A) specialists, bankers, investment brokers, and financial planners. (Most major investment banking firms won't consider participating in a merger/buyout unless your company's annual sales are more than $25 million.) A certified public accounting firm, a law firm, or a matchmaking firm with these professionals on staff can handle the entire deal for you, if you want to keep the number of third-party participants to a minimum.

Costs

In contrast to other capital-raising techniques, a merger/buyout can be relatively inexpensive to execute. Most CPA firms, for example, charge a flat fee or a set monthly retainer instead of a percentage of the sale price. At a $3 million sale price, a CPA firm would charge about $10,000 for standard accounting preparation (assuming your financial records are up-to-date and audited). The rate doubles if the firm also negotiates the sale. If a deal-broker or matchmaking firm handles the transaction, it's slightly more expensive. Many of these firms charge 5 percent of the first $1 million, 4 percent of the second, 3 percent of the third, 2 percent of the fourth, and 1 percent on every million dollars after that. If the deal is priced at more than about $10 million to $15 million, their charges are negotiated. Legal fees for the same $3 million sale would range between $50,000 and $100,000 for an evaluation of the company, legal review of your documentation, filing, and contract development. The larger the deal, the smaller the legal fee relative to the market value of the company. A third-party professional who brings you a qualified buyer usually earns a finder's fee of 1 to 5 percent of the dollar value of the transaction. Various filing fees, including Securities & Exchange Commission, NASD, state, and registrar and transfer agent fees average between $5,000 and $10,000 for a small merger/buyout.

If a buyout is financed with debt as a straight buyout or a leveraged buyout, the cost—and the risks—can be much higher. A business value lender (BVL), for example, charges 2 to 3 percent per month for a variation of an asset-based loan that values more than just the company's aggregate asset values if sold separately.

Action Plan to Access Merger/Buyout Financing

Six Months Ahead

Hire an accounting firm and a legal firm to begin the merger/buyout process on your behalf by reviewing your company's legal and financial records. It is worth the time it will take to identify, interview, and select the firms that are appropriate for your transaction, based on certain criteria: a track record in your industry, market, and form of merger/buyout; top quality business contacts; a reputation for getting top dollar; willingness to negotiate the contracts; and straightforward, negotiable fees. Inform the accountants and attorneys that you're looking for a buyer for the company. If they are pros and if the company is profitable, they will be able to recommend several buyer candidates when you are ready.

Five Months Ahead

Hire other outside experts as needed, including an investment banker if the deal is $5 million + , a valuation expert if the sale price hasn't been determined, and/or a matchmaking firm if you want someone to put the entire deal together for you.

Four Months Ahead

A legal review and financial audit should be underway in order to bring all corporate records up-to-date and to eliminate any omissions, errors, or marginal business practices, including such paperwork as lease agreements, employment contracts, rights of first refusal, shareholder or management loans, and corporate charter and bylaws. Also at this time, a prospectus must be provided if the buyer or seller is a public company. Depending on the dollar value of the two companies and on the nature of the transaction, the prospectus can be standard length or short-form.

Three Months Ahead

Target companies are evaluated by your accountants and attorneys to find a fit in terms of earnings/cash flow, assets, diversification potential, tax credits, export opportunities, compatible technology or product lines, and structural compatibility. This matchmaking process can take a variable amount of time, contingent on the quality of your buyer leads, market conditions, available financing, and many other factors. When you receive an offer, you or the buyer may have to get shareholder approval in order to execute the merger/buyout. Dissenting shareholders usually can be bought out through a buyout clause in the contract. If either party is a public company and contingent on the nature of the merger/buyout, certain SEC and state disclosure requirements may have to be met by your attorneys.

How to Time Merger/Buyout Financing

Like all equity financing strategies, a merger, sale, or buyout—
with the exception of a leveraged buyout—is more profitable for
you when interest rates are rising and/or other inflationary trends
are evident. During this phase of the economic cycle, the valuation of nearly all companies is higher and stock prices follow. It is
particularly important to time a merger or buyout when interest
rates are at their peak because that's when the value of this one-
time financing is highest. If you wait too long and interest rates
begin to fall even slightly, the valuation of your company will be
set lower. If you don't wait until rates have peaked, you'll lose
cash value when rates rise again later.

Another consideration is the health of the dollar. After the
stock market crash in 1987, the dollar was weak compared to
other currencies. That made the purchase of U.S. companies less
expensive for foreigners, who also were eager to complete mergers before the end of the Reagan administration. As a result,
foreign buyers nearly doubled their U.S. buyouts in the first half
of 1988, to $31.3 billion from $16.8 billion. They concluded 13
percent of all mergers for the same period, with Britain and
Canada at the top of the active list.

It is also important to estimate the position of the company's
industry and your local economy on the inflation-to-recession
scale. The entire nation may be prospering under inflationary
effects; but if your buyer/investor is local and the local economy
is soft, this one-time financing will generate less cash. The same
is true of the conditions in your industry. If offshore, or U.S.,
competitors threaten to dominate market share or already do,
you'll get less cash from the transaction.

Seller Protection Checklist

- All assets as collateral
- Buyer financials
- Buyer credit cards

- Security agreement and financing statement
- UCC-1 filing
- Escrow agent/attorney
- Collection agent appointment
- Sublease (site control)
- Buyer references
- Required insurance coverage: equipment, inventory
- Inspection rights
- Party to continued financial statement
- Inventory/equipment minimums
- Secondary collateral
- Personal guarantee if corporation
- Insurance payable to seller

Buyer Protection Checklist

- Signed financials
- Signed financials on listing agreement
- No pending or threatened litigation on warranty
- Contractual ability to sue for specific performance
- Owner-carry or escrow (set-off on note)
- Good personal due diligence
- Validate reason for sale
- Physical inventory: equipment, supplies
- Contract for familiarization
- Adjust price for inventory deviation
- Covenant not to compete

- Omit receivables and payables, if possible
- Seller warrants free and clear at close of escrow
- Seller universal indemnification
- Condition of equipment guaranteed
- Require all company records by contract
- Operation prior to closing clause
- Company premises
- Customer pre-payments/deposit
- Licenses/building codes/accreditation
- Work in process
- Bulk transfer

VENTURE CAPITAL

Entrepreneurs who want an infusion of new cash at the $100,000 level generally are not candidates for venture capital from a public venture capital fund, a private venture firm, a Minority Enterprise Small Business Investment Company (MESBIC), or a large corporation. Some of the lowest seed financings available for start-up companies fall in the $300,000 to $500,000 range. Occasionally, a venture capital seed fund that works in tandem with a local incubator may invest as little as $100,000 in a tenant company.

One reason traditional venture capital is hard to get unless you're raising at least $1 million is the investor emphasis on high growth potential. Companies in cutting-edge industries, emerging technological fields, or breakthrough arenas of research and development require asset/service support measured in millions of dollars, not thousands, to actualize their potential: this means you are expected to complete R&D or the prototype rapidly, identify the most lucrative global markets quickly and efficiently, and penetrate target markets long before the competition does.

To accomplish all that while delivering a superstar, profitable product requires millions of dollars. It also requires that your product or technology have the sales potential to grow beyond the level of those expenses.

Measured in real terms using the standard venture capital formula, your company must have enough growth potential to return the investors' initial investment ten times in three to five years. Venture capital firms vary in the amount of return they expect, and in the number of years they're willing to nurture a company before they cash out. Many firms want 40 to 50 percent compounded annual returns to finance a start-up or first-stage product; 30 to 40 percent compounded annual returns to back a second-stage financing; and 25 to 30 percent compounded annual returns on a third-stage deal. A 35 percent per-annum return is average. The soft small-business economy of the 1980s has softened the expectations of many venture capitalists around the country who are happy with compounded annual returns in the 25 to 30 percent range for an investment that lasts five years, on average.

There have been fewer start-ups than ever in venture capital portfolios during the mid- and late-1980s for several other reasons. Venture firms are no longer as willing to spend seven years nurturing a seed-level company through its volatile first years—the high-risk years—without a firm "exit market" available when they want to cash out. The initial public offering market, which has been a traditional exit for venture capital investors, has not rewarded assetless, young companies since 1986. About 85 percent of all start-up firms financed by some form of venture capital are sold; only 15 percent are taken public when the company matures.

Even when a venture capitalist is willing to spend the extra management time it takes to guide a start-up company, there may not be enough additional reward from the exit option to justify his "value-added" approach to helping the business. Public venture capital firms have a short life span, usually 7 to 10 years, within which to make their money and run. They have to be more efficient in picking winners within that timeframe, and they have to keep the price of their own shares propped up

Table 3.6
Cost Comparison of Domestic and Offshore Debt Sources

Source	Domestic	Offshore
Merchant bankers		
Loans	Int. + 2 points	Int. + 3 points
Lines of credit	Int. + 2 points	N/A
Private investors		
Convertibles	35%	40%
Public investors		
Commercial paper	Int. + 3 points	N/A
Commercial bankers		
Loans	Int. + 2 points	Int. + 3 points
Government	Variable interest	N/A

in order to satisfy the fund's shareholders during the life of the fund.

Another venture capital barrier for many small, young companies is the control issue. Because of the high risks inherent in financing a start-up in virtually any industry, venture capitalists expect founders to give up effective control of the company, up to about 60 percent of their equity, in exchange for first-round financing of as low as $2 million or $3 million.

Also, venture capitalists often won't pay more than 10 to 20 times the founder's price per share of stock, even on "seed deals" of $500,000 or less. This often is a major obstacle for business owners who value their shares at much higher multiples.

Table 3.7
Cost Comparison of Primary Equity Sources
(Percents are of funds raised)

Source	Commission	Legal
Stock market		
IPO	10%	10–20%
ESOP	0	10–20%
Convertibles	7–10%	5%
Individuals		
F&F	0	Minimal
Exempt offerings	7–10%	5%
Corporations		
Joint ventures/licensing and technology transfer agreements	0	3–10%
Venture capital	0	10%
Partnerships	0	10%
Merger/buyout	0	10%
U.S. merchant banks	10%	5%
Offshore		
Merchant banks	0	15–20%
Individuals	Variable	15–20%
Corporations	0	15–20%
Government	0	Minimal

Table 3.7 *(Continued)*

Source	Accounting	Financial Printer
Stock market		
IPO	10%	$5–15,000
ESOP	10%	$5–15,000
Warrants	5%	$5–15,000
Individuals		
F&F	Minimal	0
Exempt offerings	5%	$5–15,000
Corporations		
Joint ventures/licensing and technology transfer agreements	3–10%	0
Venture capital	10%	0
Partnerships	3–10%	0
Merger/buyout	3–10%	0
Offshore		
Merchant banks	15–20%	0
Private market	15–20%	0
Corporations	15–20%	0
Government	Minimal	0

Table 3.7 *(Continued)*

Source	Valuation	Filing/Reg.
Stock market		
IPO	0	SEC/$100 min., NASD/.01%, blue sky/$15,000 per state, registrar/$5,000 to $8,000
ESOP	2–8%	See IPO
Warrants	0	Determined by stock offering
Individuals		
F&F	0	0
Exempt offerings	2–8%	Determined by stock offerings; minimal
Corporations		
Joint ventures/licensing and technology transfer agreements	0	Some joint ventures
Venture capital	2–8%	0
Partnerships	2–8%	0
Merger/buyout	2–8%	0 unless one firm is publicly held
Offshore		
Merchant banks	2–8%	0
Individuals	2–8%	SEC fees determined by offering; foreign regulatory agencies
Corporations	2–8%	0
Government	0	0

CHAPTER 4

Investigating Secondary Sources of Capital

▶ **Procurement:** The obtainment by purchase or development of general-use and mission-specific goods and services by small to large private-sector companies on contract to the U.S. government. The General Services Administration (GSA) is the government's primary purchasing agent for general-use goods and services; mission-specific goods and services are contracted for by individual government agencies and departments.

▶ **Incubator:** An office park, manufacturing facility, research laboratory, warehouse, or any other structure or concept which shelters small companies, before they enter the marketplace, with below-market rent, management assistance, seed financing, shared office equipment, and/or other corporate resources.

▶ **Development Corporation:** A partnership between the private and public sectors that allows a public sector government agency or branch—or a large bank, the Small Business Administration or a venture capital fund—to use federal, state, or local funding to seed economic growth in a geographic market by investing in start-up companies.

▶ **Champion:** An incubator manager or director who provides professional management consulting services to help new owners structure the organization, plan a marketing campaign, and solicit financing; these services generally are available to incubator tenants as well as to nontenant members of the incubator network.

OUTSIDE EXPERTS

Forms

Most of the outside experts you hire to consult the company can be considered potential secondary markets for start-up financing, including accountants, management consultants, attorneys, investor relations executives, market researchers, and tax specialists, and their respective firms. In many cases, these experts have insider access to professional networking groups within an industry or area of specialization which you can't access. For example, Big Eight accounting firms that have offices around the world network continuously with private investors in Europe, Asia, and Pac Rim countries on behalf of their U.S. clients. Private networking clubs and industry associations around the country are a gold mine of names and references, including such groups as the Houston Executive Club/Houston, TX and the National Alliance of Professional and Executive Women Network, Baltimore/MD.

The more working contact these experts have with primary sources of capital, the more likely they are to know who is currently investing in small businesses like yours. To use outside experts effectively, it's important to know their exact areas of expertise and their industry specialization: they should be experts not only in your industry, but also in the form of financing you want, such as an exempt 504 offering or a loan with warrants for stock.

Many contracts for joint ventures and stock offerings between small companies and large corporations or groups of investors preclude the payment of a finder's fee to a third-party for any reason in order to avoid future litigation by the third-party which spoils the deal and/or on-going operations. Before you hire a third-party to shop investors or partners, try to find out if any corporation or individual on your candidate list insists on a direct deal.

Outside experts who successfully attract financing for start-up companies often are paid in corporate stock, plus expenses. This practice is frowned on by many equity investors who fear that too many stock-for-services giveaways in the start-up phase will deplete the authorized shares, to their disadvantage, at some point in the future. Avoid stock compensation to outside experts whenever possible, unless there is no other way to attract financing.

Two other common ways of compensating outside experts is by flat fee or by percent of financing proceeds, as agreed in a contract you and the outside expert sign before the investor is located.

The flat or percent fee can vary widely, depending on your geographic market; the development stage, track record, and desirability of your company; current economic conditions; and the trends and potential in your industry. One rule of thumb is: the less money you raise, the higher the fee as a percent of the funds raised. On a percent basis with expenses included, a financing in the $100,000 range will cost between 5 and 15 percent of the amount raised.

Resource Possibility: Richard M. Koff, Management Consultant/ Evanston, IL

Copadco Ltd./Bronxville, NY

Investor Markets

You can use the following markets in three ways: (1) as a pre-screening process by which you select potential outside experts who are qualified to look for financing on your behalf, (2) as a direct source of financing solicited by you or a third-party, and (3) as a source of leads to other capital sources for you or your outside expert to use. The key to networking effectively is to find out as much as you can from contacts: if they're not a direct source of capital, find out who invests in them, what outside experts they use, the trends in financing amounts and terms, and anything else you can elicit that will help you and your outside expert raise money for the company.

The best way to begin looking for outside experts is to solicit references from friends and colleagues whose judgment you trust. Start a candidate list with the leads they give you and then add some of your own from the following markets:

Accounting Firms

International Big Eight firms, for example, and regional firms, can access the widest range of networks on your behalf.

Certified Financial Planning Firms

These firms, which often work in tandem with such other experts as accountants and lawyers, can be a credible secondary source of financing because of their exposure to a wide range of individual and corporate clients.

Law Firms

Look for those which specialize in financing strategies for small businesses in specific industries.

Venture Capital Associations

The venture firms themselves may not qualify you as a venture capital candidate, but they network continuously with private and corporate investors who may be interested in smaller deals.

Government Agencies

Some government agencies like the U.S. Department of Commerce and the Small Business Administration are occasional secondary sources of financing as a byproduct of performing their primary functions. Both agencies have continual contact with other small businesses, some of which may be looking for a strategic partner on a project basis, in the United States or overseas.

Private Deal-Brokers

Private deal-brokers who specialize in your industry and in the form of financing you prefer. Many of them are listed as business brokers, merger/acquisition specialists, or management consultants. (Review the list at the end of this chapter.)

Investment Clubs

Investment clubs are another networking possibility because of the easy access they offer to outside experts and to other entrepreneurs. These groups frequently are sponsored by brokerage houses for the purpose of bringing investors, company owners, and analysts together to study the over-the-counter (OTC) market, small private opportunities, and specific industry trends.

Chambers of Commerce

Chambers of Commerce in larger markets conduct seminars, workshops, and educational series that bring entrepreneurs and industry experts together. A new trend that benefits business owners in a concentrated way is the chief executive officer (CEO) or entrepreneur club, which brings peers together for in-depth analyses of such management problems as accessing capital markets and strategic capitalization to meet future financing needs. Los Angeles-based TEC is one of the largest, independent CEO organizations in the country.

Industry Trade Associations

Public Relations Firms

Many investor relations/public relations firms such as LMK/New York, NY specialize in small companies

Public Management Consulting Functions

Local Offices of national economic agencies such as the U.S. Economic Development Agency

Offshore Potential

If you use outside experts to find financing, your pool of potential investors is limited by the range of contacts your expert has developed. Entrepreneurs who want offshore investors—individuals, corporations, or government agencies—should solicit outside experts who work for an international firm in the United States, who have a track record with offshore clients, or who operate in the United States as an agent of an offshore firm. Another alternative is to find a U.S. consulting firm that acts as a liaison between small U.S. firms, usually in high-tech industries, and larger, offshore corporations or government agencies.

Costs

Finder's Fee (Flat Fee)

Some outside experts will find investors for your deal in exchange for a flat fee which is negotiated before funds are solicited. A flat fee is one common form of compensation when an expert you've hired on retainer, such as an attorney or an accountant, proposes your deal to another client. The fund-raising effort is minimal, in this case, and it contributes toward your goodwill as a client. Flat fees are highly negotiable depending on the nature of your relationship with the outside expert. Most flat fees range from 2 to 8 percent of the funds raised; the finder's fee for a bank loan ranges from 1 to 5 percent or more.

Percent Fee (Commission)

Most experts prefer to raise financing in exchange for a percent of the proceeds, which ranges from 5 to 15 percent of the amount raised. Expenses generally are included in the commission, but some experts may charge an additional amount for out-of-pocket expenses related to locating or communicating with the investor. It's common to pay a higher commission when the amount raised is $100,000 or less because of the presumed difficulty in finding investors who are interested in very small deals.

Stock

Stock in the company can be used as compensation for fund-raising services, but giving away too much equity in the company in exchange for any services rendered can preclude opportunities to raise equity in the future. Investors prefer to see large blocks of stock still available, and in as few hands as possible.

Action Plan to Access Financing Through Outside Experts

One Year Ahead

If you want an outside expert to raise offshore financing, a one-year lead time isn't excessive when the competition for private equity is heating up and the trend toward economic globalization is growing rapidly. Get leads on outside experts from the professional colleagues who have used and liked their services; then interview and pre-screen several candidates before you hire him to represent the company.

After an outside expert has been selected, compile a joint list of potential investors by foreign market, by equity source, and by investor product/technology preference. Your business plan should be complete and up-to-date for review by potential investors. To accommodate foreign investors, be sure to include an extensive market analysis in the United States and overseas, as well as commentary on how your product or technology will impact their local environment. (See Chapter 2 for a complete discussion of foreign marketing.)

Hire an attorney who is a specialist in small business and in your industry to conduct a legal review of all corporate documentation. Start well in advance of the financing in case the company must be recapitalized or the corporate structure must be reorganized.

Six Months Ahead

If you want financing from investors in the United States, begin looking for an appropriate outside expert to network for financing on your behalf about six months before you need the capital. The easiest way to start is to get leads and reference names from the people you know, making sure to match the credentials and specialties of potential fund-raisers with the needs and characteristics of your company. After you have identified and interviewed two or three candidates, select one with a wide range of networking affiliations and client contacts. Compile a joint list of potential investors who are likely to be interested in the amount of your financing, your industry, and your company's prospects. Hire a legal firm to conduct a legal review of the company's contracts and documentation, and an accounting firm to update and audit its financial records. Shrewd investors will want to be sure that the company's capitalization and corporate structure are sound, and that all records and documents reflect your current operations.

One Month Ahead

Decide whether you want the legal firm to negotiate the contract for you; many entrepreneurs who acquire offshore financing consider outside negotiators a necessity when terms are decided in a foreign location and/or in a foreign language. Your legal firm should begin to write the investment contracts, including as much specific information about the financing as possible.

How to Time Financing Through Outside Experts

The movement of key economic indicators has very little affect on this form of secondary financing. Like strategic alliances that are created within primary capital markets, third-party deals tend to be created for specific purposes that cross economic conditions for the companies involved, particularly at the $100,000 level.

GOVERNMENT

Forms

Direct/Discount Loans

Loans offered directly by a government agency to qualified borrowers, often at an interest rate that is slightly lower than market rate for variable maturity periods. The borrower qualifications for a direct loan are more stringent than the requirements for a guaranteed loan.

Guaranteed Loans

Debt financing from an outside source such as a bank for 80 to 90 percent of the borrower's financial request, based on a guarantee from the government agency for the balance of the loan.

Equity Investments

Capital sourced from the private sector through a government agency; generally, it is awarded by a state-run business development entity, an R&D project under the aegis of the SBIR Phase 3 program, or a private development program sponsored by a specific government department like the Department of Defense. With a $60 billion annual budget for research and development, the federal government funnels about $20 billion into small business projects developed at approximately 700 research laboratories around the country. Despite the size of the government's annual R&D budget, small business owners and inventors should not consider the SBIR a likely source of equity capital unless you are a recognized expert in your industry, unless your company is widely acclaimed and highly unusual in some way, or unless you can back up enormous confidence in a breakthrough technology or product.

Revenue

The federal government is primarily a source of revenue for small business owners who are willing to start by raising very small amounts of capital. If you are unfamiliar with the government bidding process for either a procurement program or the SBIR program, it's a good idea to learn the bidding guidelines from someone who has bid successfully in the past. The key is to bid at an appropriate price level. You should be close to the low bidder, but bid high enough to cover your R&D expenses and provide a profit margin. Owners who become adept at winning bids for government contracts through procurement programs, for example, often build up increasing amounts of capital by completing larger and more complex projects. High-tech companies like Ophir Corporation specialize in Phase I SBIR programs in order to compete for the larger amounts of capital available through a Phase 2 or Phase 3 contract.

Investor Market

The U.S. government can be a rich source of financing in one of the forms described above if you take the time to solicit the government at the most appropriate level. In general, the federal government finances projects—created around products and technologies—that are of interest and use to itself. You must meet their specifications in all cases and there is no emphasis placed on your ability to enhance local economic development. The federal government is willing to take more risk in startup companies—as long as you qualify—because it distributes funds that are earmarked specifically for research and development. In contrast, state government is much less risk-oriented because nearly all state constitutions preclude putting public tax money into any but the most conservative investments. State-run programs focus more pointedly on your needs so that your success creates new jobs, a wider tax base, and/or long-term stability within the local community—which ultimately is the responsibility of state government, among others. State government financing programs rarely make high-risk investments in startup companies unless they are partially or totally funded by the private sector.

To put some of these funds at the disposal of companies that promise to enhance local economic development, state governments create such entities as Small Business Development Companies (SBDCs), which are partnered with the private sector and act as nonbank lending institutions. They also legislate Small Business Investment Companies (SBICs) and Minority Enterprise MESBICs in the same way to make combination debt/equity investments in qualified small businesses. Special taxes, a portion of which are earmarked for both debt and equity investments, have been passed in many states.

Another form of state-level financing is funneled to small companies through incubators, which are chartered by the state and often funded through the private sector in partnership. Municipalities also partner with the private sector to create a gestation facility for fledgling firms. (More information about incubators follows in this chapter.)

There are five groups of government programs that are accessible under U.S. law to the small business owner who wants to raise less than $100,000 in seed capital. Although these "investment programs" also advance larger amounts of debt and equity funding to qualified business owners, a certain proportion of their budgets is earmarked under a federal mandate (1) to fund small companies through special minority, handicapped, disadvantaged, gender-based, and other set-aside bidding provisions of the law, or (2) to advance special purposes of the U.S. government including the penetration of new offshore markets, the export of selected American products, or import of selected foreign products.

Small Business Investment Research Program and Related R&D/Departmental Programs (for Equity)

This program has three phases: Phase 1 provides up to $50,000 for six months of feasibility or theoretical research on projects of interest to the federal government; Phase 2 provides up to $500,000 for two years of related research and development of those projects that seem most likely to be commercialized; this funding supports prototype development and follow-on private-sector financing by the entrepreneur; Phase 3 financing is sourced entirely from the private sector to complete the commercialization process.

The following federal agencies are required by law to set aside portions of their total R&D budgets for competitive grants to small businesses through the SBIR program. They also offer equity financing for specific departmental projects: Departments of Agriculture (USDA), Defense (DOD), Education (DOED), Energy (DOE), Interior (DOI), and Transportation (DOT); National Aeronautics and Space Administration (NASA), Health and Human Services (HHS), National Science Foundation (NSF), Nuclear Regulatory Commission (NRC), and the Environmental Protection Agency (EPA).

Contract opportunities are found in *Commerce Business Daily, Requests for Proposals (RFPs),* and *Bidder's Mailing Lists,* which are available from the Department of Commerce. *Bidder's Mailing Lists* also are available from the Office of Small and Disadvantaged Business Utilization in each government department and agency. This publication covers the agency's total solicitations for goods and services. You also can request to get on a particular *Bidder's Mailing List* through these offices by completing Standard Form 129.

Export-Import Bank of the United States (Eximbank) and Related Export Financing Programs (for Debt Financing)

Eximbank is an independent federal government agency which supports U.S. exporters with financing programs that enable them to compete effectively in other countries. The agency also assists foreign firms that want to export selected products to the U.S. market. Eximbank supplements private credit sources when large amounts of funding, low rates, and/or long terms aren't available anywhere else. The agency offers several financing and guarantee programs that support U.S. exports by borrowers from both domestic and foreign companies. There are four basic Eximbank programs: direct loans, guarantees, discount loans, and export credit insurance.

The Commodity Credit Corporation (CCC) functions with the Department of Agriculture to help entrepreneurs produce and market agricultural products abroad and to development foreign markets for U.S. commodities. CCC offers cash financing for up to 36 months, as well as a barter system for special trading situations. This financing is generally available for up to 12 months; terms of up to 36 months require additional justification in your financial request.

The Overseas Private Investment Corporation (OPIC) functions from within the U.S. Treasury to make private equity and loan investments in developing nations. It offers direct loans, guarantees, investment insurance, and preinvestment information/cost-sharing to companies that are economically sound, commercially viable, and answer a market need in the host country.

Aid for International Development (AID) is an independent U.S. government corporate agency which offers specific export financing. AID prefers U.S. companies that enter into joint ventures with indigenous firms in Caribbean countries, Kenya, and Peru.

State Programs (for Debt Financing Primarily; Some Equity and Debt/Equity Combination Financing)

Virtually every state in the United States offers small business/ economic development programs, from a locally funded, private-sector development agency or a business incubator to a sophisticated, full-service agency like the U.S. Economic Development Agency that is partnered by the federal government. In many states, small business programs combine public- and private-sector support and funding.

Many states have created a very flexible financing source in the form of a Business Development Corporation (BDC, or SBDC for small business). The BDC is an important source of debt capital for small firms that create jobs to enrich the local economy. BDCs are owned either by a group of private investors who are granted a license from the state, or by the financial institutions in a town or state, and organized for financing industrial companies that have difficulty raising capital. The risk is spread among all BDC backers; interest rates vary by member institution.

Funding is advanced by the individual members and corporations in the state whose corporate mission is served by increased job creation in the area. A list of state development programs generally is available from a local or state chamber of commerce office or the state government's economic development office. It's also available from the National Council of State Legislatures in Denver.

8(a) Certification Procurement Contract and
Other Procurement Programs (for Profit)

Programs for GSA procurement, preferential procurement, military procurement, small business set-asides, labor surplus area set-asides, and procurement by other civilian agencies are detailed every week day in *Commerce Business Daily*, which is published by the Department of Commerce to announce proposed government procurements (of $50,000 or more by federal agencies, of $10,000 or more by military agencies and of $5,000 or more by civilian agencies), subcontracting leads, contract awards, sales of surplus property, and foreign business opportunities. To review a copy of *Commerce Business Daily* or to get a comprehensive list called "Doing Business with the Federal Government," which lists procurement, investment and development programs that could be potential sources of financing for your business, contact one of the Business Service Centers listed in the Appendix.

The SBA also has procurement information, which can be accessed through any of the offices listed above. The data is maintained as a computerized list of firms in its Procurement Automated Source System (PASS). Companies registered in PASS have access to more than 300 government procurement centers and to 60 primary contractors throughout the United States.

U.S. Small Business Administration (SBA) (for Debt
Funding Primarily; Some Spin-Off to the Private
Sector for Possible Equity Investment)

By Congressional mandate, the SBA provides debt financing for small-business owners who need working capital, inventory purchase funding, equipment and supplies funding, or capital for the construction/expansion of a building. The primary SBA financing arm offers two kinds of business loans: loans from private lenders, usually banks, which are guaranteed by the SBA up to

$500,000 per loan; and loans made directly by the SBA. These loans are carried at interest rates slightly below private market rates, but are available only to applicants who are unable to get private financing. The SBA uses surety bonds to provide reimbursement to an individual, company, or the government if a firm fails to complete a contract. It guarantees the surety bonds in a process that is similar to its guaranteed loan program.

Another financing arm of the SBA offers preferential loan programs for borrowers who are handicapped, low-income, energy-conservation related business owners, rural development business owners, exporters, and Employee Stock Ownership Plan (ESOP) company owners. The third financing arm is a combination debt/equity program: it licenses, regulates and lends to private firms called Small Business Investment Companies (SBICs) and Minority Enterprise Small Business Investment Companies (MESBICs), supplying equity capital as well as commercial loans to small, risky and/or high-tech companies with unusual growth potential. (MESBICs loan exclusively to minority sectors of the population and to women.)

These are federally funded private venture capital firms from which capital is available on flexible terms. To qualify for an SBIC or MESBIC loan, you must have at least $1 million in capital and agreement from the SBA to provide loans to the SBIC of up to 400 percent of available capital. Most financings average about $500,000, but smaller amounts are available if an early-stage company is located near the SBIC and otherwise qualifies.

The SBA loan guarantee program also has an Export Revolving Line of Credit (ERLC) to finance pre-export production and marketing development. It guarantees up to 90 percent of a bank revolving line of credit of up to $500,000 for as long as 18 months. To qualify, the company must be at least one year old. Another way to get SBA financing is through its Certified Development Corporation (503) program. A local area or statewide corporation or authority, which can be for-profit or not-for-profit, packages SBA, bank, state, and/or private money into a financial assistance plan for the capital improvement of existing businesses. The SBA holds the second lien on its maximum share of 40 percent participation. Every state has at least one CDC.

Offshore Potential

Offshore trading that results from government financing occurs most frequently through participation in Eximbank and similar export financing programs because these agencies were created solely to support the export of U.S. products and services. The U.S. Department of Commerce is another frequent source of offshore networking through its schedule of foreign trade missions, its solicitation of foreign corporations in the United States, and its extensive program of consulting services for small businesses that operate overseas. Participation in the SBIR program may result in offshore business, particularly in the third phase when private-sector financing is solicited from domestic and offshore sources. Entrepreneurs who patent products or technologies early in the SBIR program, during Phase 1 or 2, may apply for or receive foreign patents; this attracts interest from offshore corporations and investors, and helps you network more quickly and effectively with offshore traders.

Outside Experts

If you intend to bid for a government contract award for the first time, it's prudent to seek out the help of another entrepreneur, attorney, or accountant who has bid successfully in the past. Although the government makes several negotiating and contract-writing guides available through the SBA, these printed outlines don't cover the actual practices many owners have encountered during the bidding process—practices that you should be familiar with before you fill out the forms. It's also a good idea to hire an attorney and an accountant to do a legal and financial review of your corporate documentation before you bid on a contract.

If you win, your books and documents may be reviewed by a government auditor who has very broad disclosure rights to examine most aspects of your business. If you are bidding on an SBIR project, you may want to hire a technical consultant for six months to provide the extra technical credentials and status required by the program.

Costs

Person Hours

The highest cost to you relative to government funding is the cost per hour for the time not spent managing your business. Survey other companies by telephone to find out how long it took their managements to solicit interest, prepare financial and corporate documentation, write a business plan, and comply with government bidding/negotiation requirements.

Overhead

Many government programs require that while the contract is effective, you must continue to carry full overhead expenses, including insurance policies to protect employees, the company's delivery system, and existing inventory, among other functions of your operation.

Business Plan

You must have at least a rough draft of a business plan prepared, which can cost between $500 and $5,000 depending on how much of the plan is written by outside parties. Deduct the value of up to 100 more person-hours if you write the plan yourself.

Interest Expense

The interest paid on debt financing from the government varies from two points under prime rate to about two points over prime rate, depending on the nature of the loan and the purpose of the loan program. In addition, many government lending programs similar to Eximbank, for example, require that you pay a commitment fee of between 1/2 of 1 percent and 1 percent per annum on any unused balance of the loan.

Legal and Accounting

A quick and dirty review of your legal and financial records will cost between $1,000 and $5,000, depending on how recently your records have been audited and how organized your paperwork is.

Travel and Entertainment (T/E)

Travel expenses for trips to Washington, DC to solicit government agency contracts are highly variable, depending on the number of visits and the length of the negotiating period. Most Phase 2 and 3 SBIR negotiations, for example, require two or three visits, for a cost of about $5,000 in total.

Out-of-Pocket

Costs related to your solicitation response, including copying, long-distance telephone, and extensive mailings to outside experts, vary within a $100 to $1,000 range.

Action Plan to Access Government Financing

Six Months Ahead

An accountant and an attorney should be hired to review all corporate financial reports and legal contracts in preparation for the disclosure that will be required by the government agency financing source. Although it isn't required for the application process of most government programs, the business plan should be updated and available to the government agency upon request. Call the federal government's Business Service Center in your region to get the contact name and telephone number for the government agency you want to solicit. (See the list of Business Service Centers in the Appendix.) When you call the agency for direct information, arrange to have the weekly bulletin or pamphlet describing upcoming financial awards, loan availabilities, and/or investment programs forwarded to your company. Respond exactly as requested to the government solicitation that most closely matches the capabilities and growth potential of your company. Most government investment and award programs require about six months for a complete review of all applications. During those six months, the evaluation staff will be unavailable to bidders who want to know the status of their application. In theory, the government eventually responds to all applicants, whether they are granted a financial award or not.

If you apply for a direct loan from Eximbank, for example, the procedure is slightly different but the timing is about the same. The application must be made by letter, to which are attached the schedules and details required for a rather complete evaluation of the loan request. Eximbank negotiates a loan agreement with the interest rate contingent on market conditions at the time of application. You acknowledge your obligation by signing a loan agreement and by issuing a promissory note or other negotiable debt obligation to Eximbank. Repayment terms vary between 5 and 15 years, depending on the product and the amount of the loan.

One Month Ahead

If you want an SBA loan, take your business plan plus a revised collateral statement and a use of proceeds plan to a local banker. Ask first for a direct loan; if this request is turned down, ask to apply for the Loan Guarantee Plan or Immediate Participation Plan. If the banker approves this application, inform the SBA and fill out the set of SBA forms forwarded through the bank. During the month before your loan is granted, you may have to revise or provide other documentation—or fill out more forms, as requested by the bank or by the SBA. If you have been awarded a government investment from the SBIR program, for example, you will be notified by mail that you have a set period of time—usually one month—in which to finalize your contract bid. Although government contracts contain boiler plate contents, for the most part, and very few negotiable terms, the agency automatically provides you with a negotiating guide book. Most entrepreneurs hire an attorney to review such contract terms as ownership rights, patent protection, and distribution rights in the United States and overseas.

How to Time Government Financing

Leading economic indicators have little effect on the availability of government financing, although the size of the capital pools for such programs as Small Business Innovation Research varies to a moderate degree from year to year. The U.S. government's commitment to provide financial assistance for at least a small percentage of domestic start-up (or small) companies is worth roughly $60 billion in funding that is available annually to these firms, no matter what economic effects are created by volatile interest rates and world politics.

NETWORKS/INCUBATORS

Forms

Industrial

This incubator services industrial startup companies that require manufacturing, warehouse and distribution space in more heavily-capitalized smokestack industries. With slower and lower growth potential, these tenant companies look for an incubator that provides below-market rent, administrative services, shared equipment, management guidance, and financing, for a period of one to three years. These tenants are attractive to incubator backers because they focus on job creation for industry-displaced workers in the community who may otherwise be unemployable. Most industrial incubators are managed and funded by the private sector; very few offer venture capital seed funding to tenants.

Example: Waterbury Industrial Commons Project/Waterbury, CT

Adaptive/Public- and Private-Sector

This incubator concept is designed to meet the needs and goals of a specific geographic market, for increased new job formation, increased tax base, and the tenancy of relocated companies in desirable industries. This model often is a coalition effort between the city's private sector and local or state government which is spending federal funds to accomplish its business purposes. The adaptive structure is by far the most common of all incubator models. Many are managed and seed-funded by large corporations like Control Data Corporation to apply state-of-the-art management consulting to a community-wide, grass roots effort to improve the economic health of the local market.

Example: Business Development Center/Butte, MT

University-Based

Many state and privately owned universities now offer official incubator programs, in exchange for royalties and fees, to advanced students and entrepreneurs whose research can be further developed and/or commercialized for the public marketplace or to meet the needs of the government. The incubator relationship between the student—or an entrepreneur who contracts to work through the university—and the university is similar to a standard technical incubator, which provides technical expertise, lab facilities, supplies, and sometimes financing to help the student conclude a research and development project. In some states, universities are earning extra returns on their equipment and lab space through the use of technology transfer agreements with companies in the private sector. They earn a royalty by incubating a company of any size that needs specialized facilities.

Example: Washington State University/St. Louis, MO

Technology-Based

A high-tech incubator can be almost anything from a contract research and development laboratory in the private sector to a lab facility within a large corporation that has excess capacity in space, equipment, and expertise. This incubator model is nearly always privately owned and limited for use by high-risk, high-growth R&D companies that may not easily attract other financing.

Example: New Mexico Innovation Center/Albuquerque, NM

Without Walls

In open markets and small markets that are unable to raise the necessary start-up funds for an incubator facility to house corporate tenants, the incubator concept is applied to any business throughout the market that wants managerial assistance, limited shared equipment, and a support group composed of other entrepreneurs and champions from the established business community.

Example: Princeton Capital Corporation, Princeton, NJ

Private Nonprofit Organizations

An emerging trend in incubators is the nonprofit entity which typically is formed in small communities to achieve specific, local purposes such as job creation, new businesses, and/or a tax base increase. They solicit support from the community at the grass roots level in order to build loyalty to the business community. Often, this model is supported by a seed capital component, in the form of a $1,000-per-unit limited partnership open to investors who are subject to a minimum tax rate. Unqualified investors can contribute through the local chamber of commerce with contributions of varying amounts that are pooled and funneled to the seed fund. Because the investor population is diluted by nonventure capital limited partners, you get more lenient terms than those offered by traditional venture capitalists.

Example: Rock Hill Economic Development Corporation/Rock Hill, SC

Investor Markets

- State and local government agencies; local offices of national economic development agencies
- Large corporations, to fund an incubator or to exchange excess space and equipment for royalties
- Universities
- Real estate developers; owners of large, unleased properties such as shopping malls, warehouses, and other commercial space
- Local chambers of commerce and other business-related groups.

Offshore Potential

Most incubators don't provide the opportunity to create a strategic alliance with offshore corporations or government agencies, for financing, R&D, export, sale, or other purposes. Their goal is to give you the resources to complete your R&D and commercialize a product/service/technology from it, or to cushion your company with resources until it is healthy enough to compete in the open marketplace. In the global market, there has been a proliferation of offshore incubators in the last decade; but space in these facilities is awarded almost exclusively to local companies. The best way to access an offshore incubator is, first, to establish a strategic alliance with an incubator candidate in the foreign market you want to penetrate; then, apply for an incubator opening through your foreign partner.

Outside Experts

Attorneys

The incubator agreement between the management firm/owners and you, as well as any collateral documents related to seed financing or other special services, should be reviewed by an attorney who specializes in small businesses and in your industry. If your incubator is associated with a seed capital or venture capital fund, it's important that you understand the nature and extent of the returns your company will pay the financing entity.

Accountants

All incubator documentation should be reviewed by an accounting firm for an analysis of tax effects, special bookkeeping requirements imposed by incubator management, and/or the results of financing, if applicable. An on-going accounting system should be established within the company at the same time.

Real Estate Brokers

If you tenant in an incubator facility, compare local rates for the rental of space and facilities with the rate offered by the incubator. Most standard tenant incubators offer rates that are 10 to 25 percent below market rates.

Incubator Consulting Firms

Several national incubator consulting firms offer advice about how to select an appropriate facility to match your corporate mission, growth potential, and financial needs. These firms prepare business and operating plans, and financing packages; review tenant agreements; and often serve as liaisons between the company and seed fund management, incubator management, and corporate contacts in the public marketplace.

Examples: Pryde Roberts/Washington, DC

  Technology Centers International/Philadelphia, PA

  Job Creation Limited/Flint, MI

Costs

Outside Experts

There are very few costs associated with incubator tenancy: It will cost $500 to $1,000 to have your incubator agreement reviewed by an accountant and an attorney.

Deposit

Some incubators require that you pay one to three months' rent and/or a security deposit in advance of moving into the facility. Charges for space modification generally are negotiated before you move in, and split in some ratio between you and the incubator.

Action Plan to Access Incubator Financing

One Year Ahead

Write a business plan that maps the operation of a business that will succeed over a period of several years. Highlight the objectives that indicate you can achieve significant revenue and offer increasing employment over time, especially in a large local market. A start-up business plan should include an executive summary, specific request for assistance, business description, market analysis, product description, marketing strategy plan, manufacturing/service operational plan, distribution plan, financial data, and management background.

Six Months Ahead

Hire a management team with demonstrable credentials in the company's industry, if possible, and with a track record in the community. When the key managers are in place, begin capitalizing the company from within the local market. Incubator managers look for tenant companies that are locally owned and that are financed at least in part by the founder. Interview incubator managers about their specific goals for tenant companies to make sure those goals match your mission statement. Find out how long they incubate a tenant company, how willing they are to finance you after one year, and what growth pattern they prefer. Private, for-profit incubators traditionally have offered more follow-on financing than their public-sector counterparts.

Four Months Ahead

Request application information from two or three incubators, as well as an initial interview with the board of directors or the manager. Be prepared to submit your business plan with a cover letter individually addressed to each manager. Get to know other incubator tenants and find out how efficiently the incubator operates. Make a list of services you want included in the incubator agreement.

Two Months Ahead

A representative of the incubator may be assigned to work with you on business plan revisions that would make your company look like a more desirable tenant. Be sure to have the incubator agreement reviewed by an attorney who represents only your company.

How to Time Incubator Financing

Incubators are affected more by conditions in the local economy and by interest rates than by other key economic indicators like global competition and changes in world monetary policy. Ideally, your solicitation to a privately owned incubator would be made when interest rates are going up and other evidence of an inflationary effect already exist in the local marketplace. Incubators that offer management services and existing resources with little (or no) cash also can be solicited successfully when recessionary trends are apparent; but application criteria probably will be more stringent and accompanying seed capital opportunities may be nonexistent until interest rates rise.

CHAPTER 5

Investigating Self-Financing/Blind Pools

▶ **Accredited (Sophisticated) Investors:** Individual (retail) or institutional investors who meet SEC qualifications for minimum net worth, minimum annual compensation, and financial sophistication.

▶ **Best Efforts Underwriting:** One of three underwriter agreements, in which underwriters agree to use "best efforts" to sell your shares in a stock offering but do not agree to buy the unsold shares. Most small offerings are best-efforts deals.

▶ **Cheap Stock:** Common stock issued to certain company insiders or hired experts before a public offering at a beneficial price.

▶ **Due Diligence:** The responsibility of all parties involved in preparing and signing the registration statement in a public offering to conduct a thorough survey that serves as a basis for truthful and materially complete statements made in the registration statement.

▶ **Effective Date:** The date on which the registration statement becomes effective and actual sales begin; set by the SEC.

▶ **Foreign Corrupt Practices Act (FCPA):** The FCPA requires all public companies to maintain adequate accounting records and an adequate system of internal controls; it prohibits certain kinds of payments to specified foreign officials and politicians.

▶ **Market-Makers:** The managing underwriters and some or all of the syndicated underwriters who buy or sell your company's shares at a firm price from the public, creating sustained interest in the stock and providing aftermarket support for small issues.

▶ **Short-Swing Profits:** Profits realized by company insiders on transactions in the stock completed within a six-month period, whether or not they are based on insider information.

▶ **Tender Offer:** An offer made to gain control of another company by purchasing existing shareholders' shares.

If you are prepared to spend one full year of your time and up to $100,000 in expenses, a self-underwritten financing may be the solution when your company needs cash. You can self-finance using a variety of financial instruments, including an initial public offering (IPO) to take the company public, a limited partnership, a private placement, an exempt offering, or an Employee Stock Option Plan, among others. Self-financings can be sold to either the public market or to the private market, contingent on the financial vehicle, the amount of money requested, and the eligibility of the company.

The primary characteristic of a self-financing is its reliance on management—rather than on an underwriting firm like a brokerage house—to plan, structure, document, sell, and support an offering to raise money. One of the most common, and most difficult, self-financings is the self-underwritten IPO, which is an offering structured specifically to take a company public. An IPO changes the status of a private company to publicly held status in order to access the public capital market. The company files with the SEC for permission to sell stock to the public, which is administered under the Securities Act of 1933 requiring that the issuer company disclose certain facts about the business, results of operations, financial condition, principal shareholders, and management. Other forms of self-financing offer to sell shares to more than 35 investors in a private placement, or to sophisticated investors who become limited partners. It's important to know that self-financings in the public market entail a lot of time, preparation, and cash; self-financings in the private market frequently require almost as much time and money.

Self-financing isn't for everyone: It is grueling, time-consuming, expensive, and potentially unachievable depending on local and national market conditions, industry trends, and/or the condition of your company. Although many entrepreneurs believe they will save up to 50 percent of the going-public costs by selling a self-underwritten initial public offering, for example, they discover half-way through the arduous process that they may wind up spending more to do the offering without an underwriter. If you plan to do a self-financing in the public market, it is important to know that only about one in 100 companies that begin the going-public process actually succeed in completing the offering. That includes the companies which use the services of presumably professional underwriters. Another indication of the difficulty of selling a self-financing in the public market is the prohibition in many states against a self-underwritten IPO, although the Safe Harbor Rule grants you the right to sell one if strict compliance requirements are met.

Before you decide to try a self-financing, ask yourself:

- Are there cheaper, faster, or easier ways to raise money? What are the alternatives to public ownership?

- Is the company ready?

- Is the market ready for the company? Will it appeal to public investors?

- What are the individual and corporate tax implications of going public?

- Do you qualify as a good IPO, private placement, or limited partnership candidate? What form of financing is the company likely to attract?

- How much capital does the company really need currently and how will it be used? How much more capital will be needed in one year? In three years?

- If your self-financing creates a public company, how will the change in status affect future financing alternatives?

- Can your company/officers live with the scrutiny and disclosure required of public, and most private, ownership if the self-financing accesses the public market? (Exempt offerings in the private market usually require only a minimal amount of disclosure.)

If the answers to these questions don't dampen your enthusiasm, then a review of your new sales team may. The most important component in a self-financing is the sales team that pounds the pavement to find investors for the deal. That sales team is you and your managers, although some owners hire a brokerage firm to syndicate the deal through the company (see Table 5.1). A successful sales team knows who the best prospects are, likes to work 16 hours a day, knows how to sell itself as well as the company and product, and still manages to run the operation in its spare time. The best stock sellers know that the market accounts for 70 percent of the impact on the financing, the company's industry accounts for 20 percent, and the company itself accounts for only 10 percent.

Sophisticated, flexible financings, which can be small, are transacted efficiently when favorable market and industry conditions prevail. Successful managements know when to catch interest rates in an inflationary, upward curve—and when to bide their time until negative conditions improve.

How to Evaluate a Stock/Business Broker

- Local/regional/national reputation, references
- Credentials: education, training
- Level of market activity
- Geographical match
- Affiliations
- Small vs. large firm advantages
- Areas of specialization
- Confidentiality on initial contact
- Valuation qualifications
- Sophisticated usiness evaluation tools available
- Attorney, CPA attitude
- Upfront fee, expense requirements
- Client review of all documentation
- Aftermarket activity

Table 5.1
Cost Comparison of Self-Financings and Underwritten Financings

IPO

Legal fees	10–20%	10–20%
Accounting fees	10–20%	10–20%
Commission/discount	Up to 10%	10%
Filing fees	SEC/$100 min NASD/.01% $15,000/state	Same
Registrar fees	$5–8,000	Same
Out-of-pocket	2.5–5%	5–10%
Road show	$5,000+	$10,000+

Exempt Offerings/Convertibles

Legal fees	5%	5%
Accounting fees	5%	5%
Commission/discount	0	7–10%
Filing fees		
Registrar fees	$5–8,000	Same
Out-of-pocket	0	5–10%

Limited Partnership

Legal fees	10–20%	10–20%
Accounting fees	10%	10%
Valuation fee	2–8%	2–8%
Commission/discount	0	10%
Filing fees		
Registrar fees		
Out-of-pocket	0	2.5–5%

FOREIGN EXCHANGE

If you are considering a stock offering on a foreign exchange, it pays to watch the buying habits of American investors who react quickly to changes in the strength of the dollar overseas. In mid-1988, a strong dollar continued to cut into foreign stock market gains. Measured in local currencies, the world stock index was down only 0.2 percent in the third quarter. Through the third quarter, the world index in local currencies was up 16 percent. Translated into dollars, however, the gain was severed in half, to 8.3 percent. The stronger dollar helped spur foreign interest and provided a comfortable upturn for the capital-goods sector in West Germany. However that, in turn, drained investor interest from France. And markets in Canada, Singapore-Malaysia, and Hong Kong slipped after making good gains in the first half of 1988. The point is that stock-price movement almost anywhere on the globe—resulting from the same financial news that head-lines U.S. newspapers—affects the profitability of some companies in some markets, some industries, and some local economies somewhere. In turn, that movement can be used by companies to affect other companies, markets, industries, and economies. But as the president of a publicly held startup company, you will be hard pressed to come up with a winning strategy dealing with world financial conditions without a staff of proficient invest-ment advisors.

If you're not discouraged yet, take a look at the cost of self-financing. Contrary to conditions before 1986, it is now almost as expensive to go public on an offshore stock exchange as it is to go public in the United States.

COSTS

Person Hours

The heaviest cost related to a self-financing is the dollar value of the time spent—up to one year—by you and your managers to plan, structure, document, and sell the financing. Self-financing requires that most business owners spend almost full time on the solicitation until it's sold, which can cost the company tens of thousands of dollars in management and technical time. Multiply your cost by the number of managers involved in the solicitation and calculate whether the company can afford a self-financing based on this cost alone.

Sales Syndication

In a standard financing which requires the services of a brokerage firm, the underwriter's commission or discount falls between 7 and 10 percent of the total amount raised. Although by definition a self-financing doesn't use an underwriter, at least a portion of this discount will be paid out to stock syndicators who help you sell the financing package, or to other third parties who find investors or sell stock for you. The issue in this cost is that the discount is negotiable. It is also reviewed by the National Association of Securities Dealers (NASD)—as though it were a standard public offering—and by state securities regulators.

Legal Fees

Lawyers should be considered a critical component of your management sales team if you plan a self-underwriting. Without an underwriter to manage the preparation of the solicitation documents and other crucial paperwork, your lawyers are even more essential to the financing. They usually charge on a per-hour basis according to the financing vehicle used, the complexity of your company's legal position (relative to pending litigation, patents, and other legal issues), the amount of negotiation they conduct for you, the amount of corporate housekeeping required to get corporate records in order, and the depth of interface required by the SEC and/or state regulatory bodies. Legal fees range between 5 and 10 percent of the net proceeds.

Accounting Fees

Accounting costs also vary according to the size and complexity of the financing. Audited financial statements nearly always will be required by potential investors. If yours aren't audited, the

CPAs will spend a lot of time verifying prior years' statements. The fee includes the preparation of financial statements, the verification of financial data, and the response to SEC accounting comments. To keep this cost down, hire an auditor early in the company's life cycle so he has familiarity with the company when are ready to self-finance. Accountants bill on an hourly basis and must, by law, be paid before the completion of the offering or financing in order to be construed as "unrelated" to the company. This means they can't accept stock as payment for services, or defer payment until after the proceeds have been raised. The accounting fees will range between 5 and 10 percent of the net proceeds.

Printing Costs

This expense category can be sizeable for even small financings. It depends on how many copies of the financing document are printed, whether color is used in the materials, the length of the document, the use of art work, the number of corrections necessary, the capability of the printer, and the turnaround time. If the financing is sold in the public market, other documents in addition to the prospectus must be printed, including the registration statement, the red herring or preliminary prospectus, stock certificates, and underwriting documents, if applicable for stock syndicators. The financial printer, who should be a specialist in SEC printing requirements, will cost from 5 to 15 percent of the net proceeds.

Registration Fees

The SEC, NASD, and each state in which the offering is blue-skyed will charge an out-of-pocket registration fee or filing fee. The SEC charges .02 percent of the maximum total offering price, with a $100 minimum fee. NASD charges are .01 percent of the offering price, plus $100 up to $5,100 maximum. If the offering is registered in several states, it could cost up to $15,000 to file in each of those locations. The registrar and transfer agent fees are based on the number of certificates issued and the number of certificates transferred if there are selling shareholders. Without selling shareholders, the fee is a maximum of $5,000; with selling shareholders, add another $3,000 to the cost.

Road Show Expenses

Depending on your travel budget, you and your managers will take your company's show on the road to entice investors into your deal. Related expenses can include a professionally produced video for $25,000 to $50,000, a slide show version of the video for $8,000 to $10,000, or brochures that can cost up to $5,000 for a small quantity.

Many of these costs are high relative to the amount of financing raised, but some entrepreneurs find ways to reduce or eliminate them by careful planning. This element is the most important in the self-financing process: careful planning is mandatory if you hope to fulfill all the requirements of structuring and documenting the financing. Table 5.2 is a time/flow chart that indicates the tasks which need to be performed before the financing can be sold.

A flow chart that more realistically reflects the delays and glitches experienced by many entrepreneurs who self-finance appears on the next page, with a brief description of the financing tasks that can take up to one year to complete.

One Year Ahead

A law firm and an accounting firm should be engaged to begin the lengthy preparations usually required for a self-financing, including a corporate review of all legal documents and an audit of appropriate financial statements for perusal by potential investors. All contracts and records, financial and nonfinancial, should be clarified and "cleaned up" if necessary at this stage.

The registration statement, which is the disclosure document that contains all the information about a prospective public offering or financing, should be prepared if applicable. There are two types of disclosure required: one type is concerned only with the offering itself, the other is the continuous disclosure required

Table 5.2

Ideal Flow Chart for a Proposed Initial PublicOffering (IPO)

Date	Responsibility	Party
January 16	Planning meeting to outline the offering; assign responsibilities for schedule, format of prospectus and due diligence	All
February 23	Distribute first draft of prospectus	C/CL
Week of February 23	Prepare rough underwriting agreement, underwriters' agreement; power of attorney; underwriter's survey; survey of officers, directors and selling stockholders; rough blue-sky memorandum. Screen and select a financial printer, registrar, and transfer agent. Select banknote company to prepare stock certificates Distribute all questionnaires. Set custodian arrangements and powers of attorney for selling stockholders.	UL C C CL
February 24–25	Drafting meeting; due diligence meetings; make customer/vendor lists available	All
February 28	Distribute another draft of S-1 and underwriting agreement to appropriate staff.	CL/UL
March 1–2	Hold another drafting session; continue due diligence.	All
March 5	Distribute first printed proof of S-1 to appropriate staff.	CL
Week of March 6	Company officers, directors, and selling stockholders return surveys. Hold company board meeting to approve offering, establish a pricing strategy approve S-1 forms and underwriter's agreement. Officers, directors, and selling stockholders sign S-1 execution pages. Review possible syndicate list.	C/SS C C/SS U
March 7–8	Hold another drafting session. Review market conditions, the economy, timing of offering, and filing date. Forward revised S-1 and underwriting documentation to financial printer. Continue due diligence and cover comfort letter with accountants.	All U CL/UL U

Table 5.2 *(Continued)*

Date	Responsibility	Party
March 11	Distribute second printed S-1 proof to appropriate staff.	CL
March 14	Final working session at financial printer's office to review new proof, make final changes in S-1 and other documentation. Accountants sign report and consent from S-1.	All A
March 15	File S-1 with SEC and NASD; Issue press release.	CL/UL C/U/PR
Week of March 20	Send syndicate invitations; begin blue-sky process; consider NASDAQ listing.	U UL C/CL
Week of March 27	Launch domestic road show; hold underwriter's info meeting in New York City; write underwriter advertising; review market conditions; complete blue-sky qualification; write stockholder letter outlining reasons for stock sale; accountants distribute rough comfort letter.	C/U C/U U/PR C/SS/U UL CL A
Week of April 5	Launch offshore road show.	C/U
Week of April 19	Review returned SEC comment letter and prepare response; distribute underwriter report; do acceleration requests.	All U C/SS/U
April 20	Conduct pricing meeting; file the final amendment.	C/U UL/CL
April 21	Execute underwriting agreement and agreement among underwriters; SEC announces issue effective; begin the public offering; issue final press release re offering; distribute supplemental blue sky memorandum;	C/SS/U U U C/U UL
April 22	File 10 prospectuses with SEC; begin stabilization reporting to SEC.	C U
April 25	Provide breakdown for stock certificates; authorize registrar and transfer agent to deliver ccertificates to New York City for inspection.	U C
April 27	Preclosing; certificates available for inspection.	CL/UL C
April 28	Closing; payment and delivery; get accountants' second comfort letter; execute other closing documents.	All

Parties to the offering: Company, C; Selling stockholders, SS; Company lawyers, CL; Accountants, A; Underwriter, U; Underwriter lawyers, UL; Financial printer, FP; PR firm, PR.

after the company has become a publicly held entity. The registration statement is two sets of documents: Part I is the primary selling tool, Part II contains all the extra information required by the SEC. Both parts are considered public information and can be reviewed by anyone.

8 Months Ahead

The prospectus or offering circular, as appropriate, should be prepared. Although this document is not lengthy, its preparation is an enormous drain on management time, for researching the data required and writing the document. This document has two functions: it's a vital source of disclosed information about the positive and negative aspects of your business (it's required by the SEC to be distributed to potential investors), and it's a selling tool. The prospectus reveals summary information about the company, risk factors, financial ratios, use of proceeds, the determination of the offering price, dilution, dividend policy, if any, capitalization, properties, legal proceedings, selling security holders, management and certain other security holders, distribution plan, the interests of named experts and counsel, issuance and distribution expense, and all of the company's financial statements.

Preparations for the road show should begin at this point, to generate interest in the stock and, therefore, affect the last-minute pricing positively. You need to decide what communication tools to use from among video presentations, slide shows, red herring prospectuses, and/or leave-behind materials and brochures. You'll need to hire a communications expert in the medium you've chosen, format the presentation, write or script the presentation, complete the production, train your managers for their parts in the show, select music or background, and develop complementary artwork to round out your presentation.

6 Months Ahead

You and your managers must also register the deal in states where the financing will be sold. Each state has its own "blue sky" laws, which refers to statutes that prevent the securities-buying public from losing too much money in speculative deals. To blue-sky your issue means to analyze, investigate, and qualify the offering within these statutes. It is imperative to review the blue sky regulations for the state in which the company is headquartered and for the states where the offering will be sold. The regulations are highly variable by state, as are the filing and other related expenses (see Appendix).

3 Months Ahead

The completed registration statement and all other relevant data are submitted to the SEC, along with the filing fee and a transmittal letter that is reviewed by the Department of Corporate Finance for omissions and "misstatements." The earliest possible effective date, on which you can begin to sell your offering, is 20 days from the time your statement is reviewed by the SEC. In most cases, deficiencies within the registration statement are noted and outlined in a letter that goes to your corporate or securities attorney. Your documents will undergo either a customary, summary, cursory, or deferred review, which leaves you three ways to respond to the resulting deficiency letter: File an amended statement if the number of changes is high, make the requested revisions to the statement, or make the changes by telephone with additions or deletions written into the later pricing statement.

Between the filing date and the effective date is the waiting period or 20-day cooling off period when you must be cautious about publicizing the company. Communication about the financing or offering, or the company, should be limited to oral presentations, tombstone ads, and the preliminary prospectus. No written presentation is allowed. During this period, indications of interest in your offering are noted by the syndicators you've hired to help sell stock, but sales are not completed until after the effective date. This hiatus gives everyone a chance to predict how well it will sell, and a chance to make final changes to the registration statement.

The road show is conducted in the U.S. markets you've identified as key investor locations. The tour itinerary may also include foreign locations, to visit portfolio managers, syndicate members, securities analysts, and others who—hopefully—will develop a good impression of your company and pass it on to their stock-buying clients. The purpose of these meetings is to present the negatives as well as the positives about your company, answer extensive questions about your company or the financing, and impress your audiences favorably.

Effective Date

A pricing amendment is filed with the SEC, including deficiencies noted by the agency, the final pricing, and underwriter discount (if stock syndicators are used). Your offering then is considered effective and can be sold to the public market. The printer is notified of the changes and the final prospectus is printed and distributed to anyone who received a red herring.

Actual selling and the exchange of cash now takes place, based at first on the indications of interest gathered in the months before the effective date. In standard offerings that are underwritten by a brokerage house, managers insist on indications of interest of from 110 to 140 percent of the total offering, depending on national market conditions. This gives you an idea of the extent to which brokers pad their selling efforts with extra sales to insure against an incomplete offering during a downturn in the market, a decline in interest in the company, or an inability to sell the offering effectively without additional underwriter assistance.

At this point, tombstone ads can be produced to advertise the fact that the company is selling a security. It is important to avoid the appearance of an offer to sell stock, which is illegal, so the ads are limited to very basic information about the offering.

Six to eight days after the effective date, a preclosing meeting is held as a dress rehearsal for the final meeting after the offering has been sold out. (If the minimum number of shares has not been sold within the stated period, the deal is killed.) The closing memorandum is circulated, describing the closing process and indicating who gets original documents.

For the 90 days after closing, the company must continue to keep a low profile and hold off on announcements of new developments. Changes in the company or its financial position now must be reflected by a sticker attached to the prospectus. Companies going public or the first time must file a Form SR which shows the actual use of proceeds from the offering. This form is filed within 10 days of the end of the 90-day quiet period, continuing every six months until all proceeds have been spent.

Now that the financing has been closed successfully, the company is a publicly held entity that has further responsibilities to meet on an continuing basis. These on-going obligations are annual, costing about 50 percent of the cost of taking the company public. The very first one is stock stabilization in the aftermarket. It is crucial that your stock wind up in "strong hands" after the sale, with investors and market-makers who won't sell immediately to gain a very short-term profit on the rise that often occurs when a stock is first offered to the public. Another aftermarket safety strategy you can impose is the overallotment, or "green shoe," which allows you to sell up to 15 percent more stock than was originally planned. The intention is to cover a short position from indications of interest that didn't materialize.

Next you must decide if your stock should be exchange-listed on the New York Stock Exchange (NYSE), the American Stock Exchange (AMEX), or the Over-The-Counter (OTC) market. Most start-ups in the IPO market don't come close to qualifying for exchange listing on the NYSE or the AMEX, so they choose the OTC market, if qualified. From there, you must select whether to list on the National Market System, NASDAQ, or on the pink sheets. To be one of the 4,500 NASDAQ-listed companies in the United States, you need a corporate net worth of $1 million, corporate assets of $2 million, a minimum of 300 shareholders, at least 100,000 publicly held shares, two or more market-makers, and the ability to pay an annual fee of $2,500 or $.0005 per share.

The most onerous of the on-going duties assigned to the management of a public corporation is periodic reporting:

Form 10-K

This is filed within 90 days of the company's fiscal yearend; it includes audited financial statements for the past two years for the balance sheet, income statements, and the statement of the sources and applications of funds; a business description; revenues contributed by each major product department; a summary of operations and management discussion; a description of physical property locations; pending or actual legal proceedings, identification of subsidiaries and affiliated companies; number of shareholders; management team and remuneration; directors and remuneration; interest of management, shareholders, or directors in certain transactions.

Form 10-Q

This must be filed within 45 days of the end of each of the first three quarters of the fiscal year, including unaudited financial statements, management discussion and analysis, and information about material corporate events.

Form 8-K

This reports any changes in control of the company, mergers, acquisitions, and other significant changes in the assets, bankruptcy, receivership, independent auditor changes, and changes in management or directors.

Proxy Statements

Prior to any shareholder meeting or any vote taken, you must send shareholders a proxy statement if you are soliciting their votes, or an information statement if you are not soliciting votes. All proxy materials must be sent to the SEC 10 days prior to the date they are sent to shareholders, for review and clearance.

Schedule 13-D

Shareholders or groups of shareholders who own or control 5 percent or more of your stock or who make a tender offer for that much stock must file disclosure statements on Schedule 13-D to disclose the identity of the buyers, the source and amount of funds used to acquire the stock, the number of shares owned or controlled, and the reason for purchase.

"Short Swing" Profits

Any officer, director, or 10 percent stockholder must reveal holdings of all company securities before the offering becomes effective. Insider shareholders who both buy and sell, or sell then buy, stock within a six-month period, must give all profits to the company. These insiders also are prohibited from making short-sales of the company's securities.

Investor Relations

The only way to increase your stock price is to create more buyers than sellers. To do that, investors, both current and prospective, must be kept informed about and interested in the company through an on-going program of communication about new developments and good news. The key in investor relations is to keep your company's name before any group of investors as often and for as long as possible.

There are other hidden disadvantages to self-financing in the public market. A self-underwriting is not only the most time-consuming strategy, it's also the most expensive before, during, and after the offering. You are basically selling your shares against nearly 40,000 other listed and unlisted stocks in the after-market. Without the market maker support of a brokerage firm behind you, you have to persuade outside market-makers to up-hold trading so that there is a market in the stock that will yield profits in the future.

Another disadvantage is that insider, or control, shareholders—also called 144 shareholders—aren't allowed to sell their shares for two years due to stringent SEC regulations.

HOW TO SELF-FINANCE MORE EFFICIENTLY FOR LESS MONEY

- Hire a brokerage firm or stockbroker as a stock syndicator who works for you on contract. Make sure the commission or discount percent is less than the 10 percent you would pay an underwriting firm. (When you hire an underwriter, you also pay its legal fees, upfront expenses, and certain out-of-pocket costs designated by them—all strategies to transfer some of the financial risk in the deal to you.) When you and your managers function as the lead salesmen for the offering, you have more control over the terms of the offering, including the pricing of the shares.

- Retain continuity in the legal function by combining the offering and the corporate counsel functions: This individual counsel performs a corporate review during the "house-cleaning" phase of preparing the offering, and acts as your advisor during and after the offering. These functions demand that the attorney be a specialist in securities, in your industry, and in small offerings.

- Obtain unofficial "indications of interest" long before the preparation process begins, so that initial selling efforts result from "sure" sales. It's difficult to reach public investors during the two quiet periods before and after the offering, so every effort should be made by you and your managers to gain their attention well in advance of the quiet periods.

- Don't try to self-finance during a critical phase in your company or product development cycle. Time the offering for a period when you project there won't be fires to put out, major decisions that have to be made, or economic conditions that will make the offering more difficult to sell. Plan to devote nearly all of your corporate time to the financing so that it can be sold out within the allotted period.

- Keep the legal documents, including the prospectus or offering circular, as simple and inexpensive as possible. Investors in small deals tend to favor materials that are produced on a low budget because they're an indication of management's desire not to impress anyone and its ability to hold down costs.

- Talk to other entrepreneurs who have completed a similar self-financing to get the real-world picture of what the process entails. Also talk to underwriting firms to pick up suggestions about how to streamline the procedure, how to interpret SEC responses, and how to attract secondary syndication interest (sales support) from brokers.

- Interview potential market-makers from among the brokerage firms to identify and solicit support from the underwriting firms that will prop up your stock in the aftermarket. One of the primary reasons small companies fail in the public market is that, having completed an offering, their shares aren't supported by market-makers for long-term investing. This means a cadre of five or ten loyal firms should be enlisted to hold bulk amounts of your stock at favorable prices to keep investor-interest high. These market-makers should insure that your shares are easily bought and sold through them, and that their pricing is favorable: the bid/ask spread shouldn't be too great, and the price should be maintained or bumped up when investor interest is high.

REVERSE ACQUISITIONS: BLIND POOL OR BLANK-CHECK COMPANIES

To utilize a blind pool, you can merge (exchange stock) with a blind pool or blank-check company. The pool is an amount of cash available from a cash-rich company formed specifically to merge with an existing, cash-poor, private company like yours. Usually the blind pool company raises money in the public market after filing a registration statement with the SEC. The blind pool sells its common stock, along with warrants to buy additional stock at a premium over the market price. At that point in time, the blind pool company merges with your private company. You get the cash raised by the blind pool company, and the blind pool stock is transferred to your shareholders in exchange for stock in your company in some negotiated ratio. In this way, your shareholders own the majority of the outstanding stock of the public blind pool, which transforms your private firm into a publicly held corporation. Although this transaction is often referred to as a merger, the SEC's technical name for it is "reverse acquisition."

A blind pool offering is potentially beneficial because, at least theoretically, it offers immediate cash, future cash through the exercise of attached warrants, and the status of being a publicly held company. In the same way, a blind pool works like a shell company merger, which has been around for years in the oil and gas, and other, industries. A shell company has discontinued operations, may or may not have the cash you're looking for, and is a publicly held corporate entity.

These are enticing advantages to a small business. In addition, many investment brokers suggest that a blind pool offering is cheaper than an IPO and requires less time to comply with SEC red tape. But most blind pool offerings net far less cash to a private company, as a percent of net proceeds. They take more time to prepare, sell, and support in the aftermarket than cash-poor owners acknowledge, and the expenses related to this strategy often exceed everyone's expectations. The key element that determines success in a blind pool offering is the quality of the blind pool management. These offerings have suffered in the past from the same perception investors have of certain pink-sheet or OTC stocks: the companies are all hype and their managements are in place only to make a quick buck at the market's expense.

Blind pools frequently are sold by inexperienced or unethical managements that have been known to raise just enough capital to pay themselves a large salary, with very little left over for the company after expenses. Many states have passed legislation banning the sale of blind pool offerings.

If you consider a blind pool offering, investigate the compliance required under federal and state government reporting/disclosure regulations. Among other documents, you must provide accounting information that is time consuming and expensive to prepare, including:

- Audited financial statements for the blind pool company

- Audited financial statements for the private company (yours)

- Pro forma financial statements for the stock exchange transaction and combined entities

- Full disclosure of blind pool operations through due diligence

- Full disclosure of private company operations through due diligence

You don't have to prepare a prospectus, which is required for an initial public offering, for example, but you do have to develop a post-effective amendment—which is almost as detailed and expensive to produce. Combined, the preparation of these filings can cost up to $20,000 in legal and filing fees during the first 12 months.

If the blind pool deal is a unit offering that includes warrants to buy stock at a later date, don't count on warrant proceeds if the market price of your stock is depressed because of poor operating or market conditions.

The cost of doing a blind pool offering isn't necessarily lower than the expenses related to other public or private offerings. This financing can require extensive legal and accounting work if your company documentation isn't cleaned up and up-to-date. If the company's financial statements have not been audited or reviewed previously, that task will have to be completed before the offering can be sold.

In addition, you will start accruing on-going reporting/disclosure costs immediately after the date your offering becomes effective. When the registration becomes effective, you have an obligation under the 1934 Securities Act to begin reporting company operations by filing Forms 10K, 10Q, and 8K. Form 8K alone requires two years of balance sheets and three years of income statements, statements of cash flows, and statements of changes in stockholders' equity.

CHAPTER 6

Balancing Debt and Equity

- ▸ **Capital Structure (Capitalization):** The company's financial skeleton, including preferred stock, long-term debt, and net worth. It is distinguished from the financial structure, which includes other sources of capital such as short-term debt, accounts payable, and other liabilities. Capital structure is measured by the debt/equity ratio, or leverage.

- ▸ **Convertible Debenture (Hybrid Security):** A debt instrument that can be converted to stock at a prearranged price for a designated period of time, up to perpetuity.

- ▸ **Dilution:** The impact on earnings per share and book value per share if all convertible securities are converted, or if all warrants or stock options are exercised.

- ▸ **Senior Debt:** Debt instruments, including loans, that are repaid before junior debt or equity.

- ▸ **Unit:** Relative to securities, a unit is generally two or more classes of securities offered together such as one common share and one subscription warrant are sold as one unit of stock.

- ▸ **Warrant:** A security issued with a stock or bond that allows the shareholder to buy a certain number of common shares at a set price for a specific period of time.

Most start-up entrepreneurs try to operate their companies with corporate strategies that evolve from SOP management, or seat-of-the-pants decision-making based on someone else's conditions and timing. Once his product is brought to market and the cash clock is ticking, there is seldom enough time to create and execute a capital strategy, for example, that will support other corporate goals. But if you put off the creation of it long enough, the capital structure on which your company depends will be determined for you by the needs of the marketplace and by the needs of your competitors.

The idea behind an appropriate capital strategy is to establish a balance between the amount of debt carried by the company and the amount of equity in the business. If you have sold too many shares of the company to insiders and early investors, and to third-party professionals in exchange for their services, later investors will turn down your financing request because ownership is too diverse. Conversely, if you've borrowed more money than the company can realistically pay back, investors will avoid the company as a high-risk investment.

The pivot point where debt and equity are balanced is different for every business, but its importance is the same: the capital structure determines your financial health and your ability to raise capital when you need it. As the company grows, your capital structure determines the price and value of your stock, how accessible debt and equity capital will be in the future and how competitive you'll be relative to your resources.

This means it's crucial to plan the scope and nature of every round of financing up to and including the exit strategy—merger, IPO, sale, or ESOP, for example—by which you and your investors cash out of the company.

One way to take control of your capital structure is to set a universal financial goal, then amplify that goal with the specific requirements that arise from your company's position in the market. Start by deciding that your financial goal is to insure that capital will be available under all conditions, at a cost you can afford, when you decide to expand. This means you'll be able to finance the business adequately under all adverse conditions:

- When there are problems in the economy like recession or inflation
- When there's a crisis in the securities market
- When there's a problem in your industry
- When the company has problems

Against this backdrop of adverse conditions, from which seasoned entrepreneurs always select one or two as likely possibilities, decide how much fund-raising latitude the company should have. There are five components of future capital availability that will emerge if the company matures successfully:

1. The ability to raise money anytime. Ideally, you'd like to insure that you can raise money no matter what the market is doing and no matter how low your earnings are.

2. The ability to raise money without hurting the company's credit rating. You can pull the company's credit rating out of the fire, but it's a long, expensive, no-growth process.

3. The ability to raise money at the lowest cost in order to generate long-term stockholder returns. This component demands that the company avoid high rates and restrictive terms in senior capital or securities, expensive equity kickers like convertibles and warrants, the sale of common stock when the price is down, and the necessity for high returns because of unnecessary risk to the common stock.

4. The ability to generate a quality common stock. This means a gradual increase in earnings per share as the common stock investment increases through retained earnings. As your price/earnings ratio stabilizes, there should be long-term appreciation in the price of your stock (later-stage companies).

5. The ability to pay dividends that won't have to be cut back or eliminated for financial reasons (later-stage companies).

The most important influence on your company's ability to raise money anytime under all conditions is its ability to sell debt in the form of loans or bonds. Remember that when lenders/ investors perceive that your capital structure is balanced without too much leverage and earnings are on track, debt financing is almost always available in some form. But if your capital structure is too rigid because of excessive debt, you will have to reduce that debt level using one of four strategies in order to satisfy hesitant investors:

1. Build up equity from retained earnings.

2. Reduce cash from internal cash.

3. Sell common stock to build up equity when the market is favorable. (If the proceeds are used to pay off debt, it can result in the dilution of earnings per share.)

4. Sell assets.

You will also have to address certain overt and hidden risks that potential lenders/investors will try to assess before they put money into the company. One of the overt risks, of course, is the business itself. They will look at your industry and your position in the industry, your vulnerability to industry fluctuations, and trends. They will look at the financial risk generated by management when the debt ratio is too high. When you pile on debt past the corporate breaking point, investment in your company becomes speculative. This increases your cost of money and adds a risk component to invest in your common stock because it has become "junior" to the new debt. The new debt is riskier, too, which increases the returns that shareholders require. Investors also will rate your history of credibility: do you tell the bad news as quickly and effectively as the good news?

Next, lenders/investors will determine the quality of credit your company deserves based on earnings, assets/liquid assets, current debt, and track record of steady increases in sales and earnings. These elements of debt quality are translated into bond ratings that describe the company's financial flexibility, or its borrowing reserve and financial insurance.

RATING YOUR DEBT TO DETERMINE
CAPITAL STRUCTURE STRATEGY

The following ratings are used to rate debt.

- AAA   The highest financial strength, achieved by only a few companies

- AA   High quality debt, usually granted to large companies that use a significant amount of debt financing; provides financial insurance

- A   Fair quality debt, lacking financial insurance; usually the highest rating given industrial companies

- BBB   Lacking in quality

- BB   Poor quality

The next step is to translate your bond rating into a ratio of long-term debt to total long-term capital. This entails a statistical comparison with similar companies with rated bonds, including all the financial ratios used to depict the bond quality for the type of company, a complete review of the company's financial statements, and an analysis of all the factors that affect the company's earning power and variability. The most important fundamental ratios are long-term debt as a percent of total long-term capital, and the number of times interest charges are earned. *It is usually earnings—their amount, volatility, and vulnerability to decrease—which negatively affects the bond rating.* For that reason, the number of times interest is earned is the most significant ratio in the analysis. Therefore, a company with a low level of debt may have an impressive balance sheet; but if earnings are poor and/or erratic, the debt will be down-rated.

For small businesses, improving debt quality is an uphill battle because most lenders/investors believe that size affects risk. They also believe that a small business is more vulnerable to negative market and economic factors that affect sales and expenses and that affect the few key people who run the business. Therefore, small companies generally are low-rated even if they have a relatively lower level of debt, and they pay higher interest charges.

This means you should not establish average and maximum debt ratios for your small business based on its bond rating alone. Instead, set the average and maximum debt ratios as if the company were large. If you reach for the A rating as a large company, you may get a credible BBB rating. If you reach for the BBB rating, you may get rated BB—but most small businesses have no bond rating at all, so you are still ahead of the game.

If your business is privately owned now but you may want to take it public in a few years, it's advisable to plan financial growth as though the company were publicly-owned today. As an IPO, your company will be evaluated on past financials. Make them conform as nearly as possible to investor expectations of a public company when the offering is made in order to complete a more successful, and profitable, stock sale.

There are five factors to consider before you and your chief financial officer actually map out your corporate debt strategy:

1. *Financial Need:* How much does the company really need, including such things as marketing support and insurance coverage? What happens if you defer the financing of these needs?

2. *Capital Sources:* Which capital sources can the company realistically access? How much of the financial need can be funded with internally generated cash without risking necessary cash outlays?

3. *Lending Requirements:* What are your company's operational and competitive risks? How will they determine the level of debt capacity and the participation of debt investors?

4. *The Competition:* Is your company threatened by competitors? If you don't receive debt financing, will you lose market share to competitors who do?

5. *Debt Policy:* Is your proposed debt strategy doable now? In five years? What other financing options will the company be able to access in the future? What operating strategies are you willing to change in order to implement or maintain your debt strategy such as compensation? Dividends?

Next are listed some of the most common debt strategies for a small business.

Return on Investment (ROI) Option

This strategy allows you to procure long-term debt when return on investment is high enough to pay back the loan. If you're going to buy new equipment to lower production costs significantly, you could get a loan financed totally by these savings. This same strategy applies to an investment opportunity as long as ROI services the debt.

Percent of Capitalization Option

Compare the company's debt principal to owners' equity and set a debt ceiling based on the balance sheet debt/equity ratio. This key ratio usually is expressed with long-term debt as a percent of total capitalization, which is common and preferred stock, and surplus accounts. This option allows you precise measurement: allowable debt isn't subjective, yet debt can increase as owners' equity increases through the retention of earnings. The downside is twofold: this option can be too inflexible, disallowing more debt even when potential rewards are promising. Companies tend to base their debt/equity ratios on their competitors' ratios, which isn't realistic even when the companies are similar or are in the same industry.

Full-Tilt Borrowing Option

This option throws the responsibility for risk assessment to lenders, who presumably will cut off financing when the debt load is too burdensome. The problem is, you may not be informed of impending problems or the approach of your credit limit until it's too late to finance the correction of a problem or take advantage of an opportunity.

No-Debt Option

Some companies avoid long-term entirely, which certainly eliminates the need for risk evaluation and contributes to your peace of mind. But when you rely on internally generated funding alone for such opportunities as corporate expansion or the penetration of new markets, there will be opportunities you'll have to pass up—losing profits and momentum—if your timing is off. Also, if the cash isn't there when you need new equipment, for example, the long-term consequences in increased costs and reduced efficiency against competitors can be even higher.

Cash Flow Analysis Option

This strategy analyzes the potential ramifications of negative cash flow in the near future and the effect of new debt added to that possibility. Because projections of future cash flow by definition are uncertain, management always subjects the company to some level of risk with any debt strategy. Therefore, projected cash flow is the most important and sensitive data factored into your debt strategy. Worst- to best-cash scenarios, including general or industry recessions, should be included over the term of the proposed loan. These possibilities should be based on both optimistic and pessimistic events which estimate how much cash will be available. The last step is to justify a realistic monthly outlay relative to the risks. Many experts feel that cash flow shows only the company's ability to repay debt, not necessarily its ability to raise new financing. And cash flow can be deceptive: if the company has strong cash flow due to large noncash items like high depreciation, it won't have financial strength without strong earnings. It's earning power after depreciation that carries the most weight in determining quality. Without earnings, the company eventually won't be able to raise common equity, which is one of the bases for financial strength.

Interest Rate Option

An easy way to set debt strategy is to declare an interest rate limit, based on the prime rate plus percentage points and excluding all debt financing above that limit. This looks like a viable strategy because the belief is that lenders will loan money at this rate only to firms with a high credit rating. However, the interest rate option places the risk evaluation burden on the lender and excludes debt financing when a higher risk can be compensated by higher returns.

Bond Rating Option

Used primarily by public companies, this strategy bases the amount of debt funding on how additional debt would adversely affect the company's bond rating. For example, the company would set a value, say "AA," for its bond rating. This rating becomes the benchmark against which all future debt activity is measured. If a potential debt financing threatens the "AA" rating now or in the future, the debt action would be dropped.

One-Time-Only Option

If your company experiences seasonal, cyclical, or intermittent swings in sales and earnings that are too severe for continued debt financing, the one-time-only option for a single project may be effective. You may have an opportunity to make a strategic acquisition and need the funds to finance the transaction. This is a justifiable, low-risk project which should be considered separately from the often expensive long-term financing of business operations in general.

Principal and Interest Option

This option curtails the size of the debt by putting a limit on the amount of principal and interest paid on the loan. This limit can be a maximum level of earnings set aside for debt servicing. Usually the limit is expressed as a ratio of earnings to payments such as earnings at two or three times the level of payments. The value of the ratio is an estimate of the projected average level of future earnings, which is based on the most current earnings. This option, then, automatically adjusts the debt limit because of the changes in earnings. It's a good, long-term approach that builds in flexibility proportional to the changes in income.

WARRANTS

One important way for a small company to correct a debt imbalance in its capital structure is to issue warrants on the common or preferred stock. This is done frequently on a debt issue or loan, part of which is convertible to equity near the end of the payout period.

A warrant is a shareholder or creditor claim to buy a specified amount of your company's common or preferred stock at a pre-negotiated price before a specified expiration date. A warrant is actually an inducement for lenders/investors who either want equity participation in what they hope is a growing company or who want to buy a $10 stock for $5 a share. They are betting the price of the stock will rise higher in the market than their warrant price. If the stock price goes down, conversely, warrant-holders would pay $10 for a $5 share of stock. When that happens, most warrant holders let the term of the warrants expire without making the investment.

If your company is publicly held and the stock price is rising, or if your privately held start-up has good prospects, the staged sale of warrants can be an effective way to cover debt repayment and keep your company's debt/equity ratio in balance. In either case, the warrant exercise period should be timed to your debt repayment schedule so that when warrant-holders exercise their options to buy stock, they provide staged equity financing with which to make the loan payments. At the same time, the exercise of the warrants automatically tips the debt/equity ratio from excess debt to a 1:1 balance.

There are two types of warrants. A subscription warrant, also called a stock-purchase warrant or a rights offering, is sold to existing shareholders who want to buy more stock at a cheaper price in the future. As an offering, this financing strategy is fast and cheap for the company. Other warrants with a longer life, up to perpetuity, are sold as an inducement to new investors.

Selling warrants is a versatile strategy because they can be packaged specifically to meet your company's capital needs. They can be combined as a unit with a senior bond, which creates a convertible or hybrid security for both debt and equity financing. If they're packaged with preferred stock, they can be priced at a premium instead of at par. They also can be packaged with common stock. And, they can be sold separately as a privately-held issue for equity financing alone.

There are specific conditions under which you should consider offering warrants. Primarily, they should accompany a debt issue or loan when the company needs capital but private lenders/investors aren't interested unless you offer this equity kicker. Another good time is when interest rates go up and it's a buyer's market for lenders/investors. Your equity kicker will distinguish you within the universe of competitors for debt financing. If you feel secure about a projected earnings increase, your warrants will look good to investors who want extra assurance that cash flow will be there to pay back the debt financing. Warrants also sell well in the IPO and secondary market when stock alone won't interest investors, when the company has a low or no bond rating, and when competition in the bond market is particularly strong.

Although the sale of warrants can be a sensitive tool for balancing your debt/equity ratio and raising small amounts of capital on a scheduled basis, there are some drawbacks to this security. Only about half of the units that package warrants for small, low-priced issues are ever exercised. This trend makes warrants a high-risk strategy as a source of capital. Also, the inappropriate sale of warrants to underwriters and/or outside experts in exchange for services rendered to the company can be a disastrous call on public stock if the market price starts to rise. Warrants should not be used to help the underwriter sell the issue or to substitute as cash compensation from the proceeds of the sale.

HOW INVESTORS AND STOCK ANALYSTS ESTABLISH THE VALUE OF YOUR MANUFACTURING COMPANY

Sophisticated investors and securities analysts have found that the financial condition of manufacturing companies is easily discerned when certain line items from the income statement and balance sheet are combined as ratios. These seven ratios have emerged as the "7 Keys to Value."

Operating Profit Margins

Profit before interest and taxes, and expressed as a percent of sales, is the most important indicator of operational efficiency in your company. Profit usually increases and declines more quickly by percent than sales because of costs such as interest, rent, and real property taxes are fixed and don't rise or fall with changes in volume.

Working Capital Ratios

This is the current ratio, or the ratio of current assets to current liabilities. A gradual increase usually indicates a improving financial strength. But if the ratio is more than 4 or 5 to 1, it's considered excessive and may signal a contraction in the business, underutilization of cash to expand operations, or stagnant inventories.

Liquidity Ratios

This is the "quick assets" ratio for cash and equivalent (marketable securities) to total current liabilities; it's also called the "acid test" ratio. It supplements the current ratio because your company may not be in a good position to meet current obligations (or pay larger dividends) despite a high current ratio. This ratio usually declines during expansion and rising prices because of heavier capital expenditures and larger accounts payable. If the decline persists, the company may have to raise additional capital.

Capitalization Ratios

These are the percents of total investment capital by long-term debt, preferred stock, common stock, and surplus. Your capitalization depends on the industry, the financial position and policy. (Relatively stable industries like utilities usually have a higher proportion of debt than manufacturing industries.) The higher the ratio of common stock and surplus, the fewer the prior claims on the company.

Sales to Fixed Assets

Dividing annual sales by the value of plant and equipment yields a ratio that helps indicate whether funds are invested productively in plants and equipment. If an expansion in facilities doesn't produce a larger sales volume, there may be a weakness in marketing strategy.

Sales to Inventories

This ratio also is called "inventory turnover" because it indicates how many times your inventory turns over in a one-year period. A high ratio signifies well-selected merchandise that is readily accessible and well-priced.

Net Income to Net Worth (Return on Equity)

Net income as a percent of the total of preferred and common stock and surplus indicates how much the company is earning on the shareholders' investment. A large or growing ratio is favorable; an extremely high ratio may invite intense competition. Also, rising commodity prices can produce temporary inventory profits. A higher rate can be due to general prosperity; conversely, a decline can be attributed to recession or less favorable conditions, as well as to higher taxes. Outlays for a new plant and equipment should yield an annual return in excess of the cost of money, if borrowing is required, or in excess of the interest on more secure investments if surplus cash is used.

CHAPTER 7

Raising $0
to $100,000

In this chapter, we have provided the resources for developing a five-step action plan for raising $100,000 or less.

WHERE TO START

First, determine how much capital realistically is available to you from debt and equity sources that are willing to finance your business with $100,000 or less.

Capital Range of Start-Up Debt and Equity Sources

Public Market

IPO	Usually $500,000 minimum; $100,000 if self-underwritten
ESOP	$100,000+; variable
Warrants	$0 to $100,000; contingent on stock price increase

Individuals

F&F	$0–$100,000; variable
Exempt offerings	$100,000+; less if self-written
Convertible securities	$100,000+; less if self-written

Lenders

Commercial bank loans	$100,000+ if qualified
LBOs	$100,000+ if qualified
Finance companies	$100,000+; variable; if qualified by assets

Corporations

Venture capital	Usually $500,000 minimum; $100,000 from incubator funds

| Joint ventures/licensing/ technology transfer agreements | $50,000+; highly variable |

Partnerships — Highly variable; includes noncash resources
Mergers/buyouts — Highly variable

Offshore
Merchant banks — $100,000+ if qualified
Private market — $100,000+
Corporations — Highly variable

Government — $50,000 (SBIR program)

Nonpublic Sources of Equity Capital

Terms	*Form: R&D Partnerships*
Amount	Varies from $100,000 to $20 million for public partnerships
Cost	Less than debt/more than equity; varies due to market conditions and project success
Structure	Tax-driven structure: early tax write-offs, later capital gains to investors
Purpose	To fund new-product research, share risk with investors, and company can't use all the tax advantages
Advantages	Attracts high-risk funding from outside investors
Disadvantages	Costs to company escalate if project successful

	Form: Venture Capital
Amount	Traditional: $500,000 and above; seed and incubator funds: $100,000 to $300,000
Cost	About 35% per-annum, compounded returns or five to 10 times initial invest-in five years
Structure	Varies by venture fund; usually preferred stock
Purpose	To support high-growth companies that will grow to $50-$100 million in five years and will go public
Advantages	Company gets risk capital, and contacts and experience from investors
Disadvantages	Company must investor growth expectations and go public as soon as possible

	Form: SBIR Grants
Amount	$50,000 to $500,000 from government and private sector
Cost	Practically none: preparation of a well-researched bid response
Structure	Federal agency or department grant
Purpose	To provide seed capital, contacts
Advantages	No equity give-up to investors; low or no cost to company
Disadvantages	Limited funding in Phase I; little or no negotiation of government contract

Form: Small Business Investment Companies (SBDCs)

Amount	Usually $100,000 to $1 million
Cost	Rate of interest, or dividend and equity participation by investors
Structure	Straight debt to straight equity; most common form is convertible (hybrid) security, either convertible debt or subordinated debt with warrants to buy common stock
Purpose	To provide expansion capital, working capital, acquisition funds, or LBO funds
Advantages	Provides subordinated capital which strengthens borrowing capacity; by law, maturity must be at least five years; interest rates are fixed
Disadvantages	Equity give-up required; must go public within three to five years; investor influence possible on board

Form: Minority Enterprise Small Busines Investment Companies

Amount	Varies by MESBIC, within $100,000 to $1 million range; available only to minority-owned businesses
Cost	Rate of interest, or dividend and equity participation in business
Structure	Straight debt to straight equity; most common is convertible (hybrid) security: convertible debt or subordinated debt with warrants to buy common stock
Purpose	Start-up, working, or expansion capital, acquisition or LBO funding
Advantages	Risk/equity capital for minority-owned firms; strengthens borrowing capacity with subordinated capital; interest rates are fixed
Disadvantages	Equity give-up required; investor-influence on company; must go public within three to five years

Form: Private Placements

Amount	$100,000 and above
Cost	Almost as much as a similar-sized IPO, or up to 20% of offering proceeds
Structure	SEC-exempt offering to designated sectors of the private market
Purpose	Start-up, working or expansion capital
Advantages	Few reporting/disclosure requirements; less costly than an IPO; can sell locally or nationally
Disadvantages	More costly than private debt and most other equity strategies; extensive legal and accounting preparation required

Nonpublic Sources of Debt Capital

Source: Commercial Banks

Amount	$100,000 and above
Cost	Usually a floating interest rate based on prime rate plus up to 4 percentage points, depending on company's borrowing capacity and risk level

Maturity	Variable including 90-day demand notes, lines of credit of from 1 to 3 years, 3- to 5-year intermediate-term loans, and long-term mortgages.
Collateral	Unsecured, floating liens or liens on specific assets; personal guarantees
Purpose	Working capital, expansion, machinery/equipment purchase
Advantages	Low-cost capital provider; long-term relationship possible
Disadvantages	Avoid start-up firms; require personal collateral and guarantees; not interested unless cash flow is strong and stable

Source: Commercial Finance Companies

Amount	$100,000 and above
Cost	Usually a floating interest rate based on prime rate plus up to 6 percentage points
Maturity	1- to 8-year revolving credit agreement; (depending on loan size: the bigger the loan, the longer the maturity) term loans of up to 10 years
Collateral	First lien on financed assets; personal guarantees usually required
Purpose	Working capital; acquisition funds; or purchase of equipment, machinery or real estate
Advantages	Lend generously against balance sheet collateral; finance high-risk companies; flexible revolving credit to fit expanding asset base
Disadvantages	High rates; borrower repays if asset base shrinks; will liquidate quickly in negative conditions

Source: Leasing Companies

Amount	$100,000 and above
Cost	Prime rate plus up to 6 percentage points; tax-advantaged leases can be less costly
Maturity	Varies by asset leased; operating leases are short-term up to several months; financing leases are effective during the life of the asset
Collateral	Secured lending with lessor retention of asset title
Purpose	Machinery/equipment, real estate, acquisitions
Advantages	Easy strategy to use; 100 percent of the asset can be funded; ownership risk lies with lessor; some tax benefits pass through to company
Disadvantages	High cost; ownership benefits like depreciation retained by lessor

Source: Life Insurance Companies

Amount	$100,000 and above; some pension funds set $1 million or more minimums
Cost	Usually fixed interest rate pegged to (lower) long-term market rates
Maturity	Ranges between five years and 10 to 25 years contingent on use of proceeds
Collateral	Unsecured debentures for financially strong borrowers; secured for asset acquisition
Purpose	Equipment and machinery, real estate, long-term working capital support

Advantages	Long-term capital; market interest rate
Disadvantages	Some minimum loan amounts are as high as $1 million; restrictive terms usually required

Source: Small Business Administration (SBA)

Amount	$50,000+
Cost	Floating or fixed interest rate subject to government-imposed ceiling
Maturity	7 to 25 years, contingent on use of proceeds
Collateral	Usually secured by floating liens on specific collateral; personal owner guarantees required
Purpose	To fund otherwise unbankable firms with working capital; to fund purchase of machinery and equipment, and real estate
Advantages	Cost to company not tied to risk level; almost any asset financable; lender of last resort
Disadvantages	All-inclusive liens required; major stockholder guarantees required; company must qualify

Source: Savings & Loan Associations

Amount	$100,000+
Cost	Fixed or variable interest rate tied to long-term market rates; working capital loans: floating rate tied to prime rate, priced commensurate to local commercial banks
Maturity	Usually 15-year, long-term; lines of credit sometimes available
Collateral	Secured
Purpose	Real estate purchase; some working capital and equipment purchase funding possible, if qualified
Advantages	Good rates available; good loan to asset ratios
Disadvantages	Better as a real estate lender; prefer strongly capitalized, stable businesses; close scrutiny of commercial firms for working capital funding

Source: Leveraged Buyouts (LBOs)

Amount	$100,000+
Cost	Usually a floating interest rate plus up to three percentage points
Maturity	Usually intermediate-term, up to 15 years
Collateral	Company's existing cash flow; asset base
Purpose	To acquire a business or asset group using more debt and less equity; to increase returns on investor capital by averaging equity infusion with a large amount of debt
Advantages	Easy debt repayment with existing cash flow; requires little equity; management familiar with operation; flexible sources including commercial banks and asset-based lenders
Disadvantages	Debt repayment vulnerable to cyclicality; may have to sell assets

Next, determine what the debt/equity source considers a good investment risk. Ask specifically for their investment qualifications or guidelines, and match them with your operation.

IPOs

IPO investors like companies with $5 to $10 million in annual revenues, at least 10 percent earnings, a unique position or market niche in a growing industry, high sales growth potential, a well-rounded management team, an asset base, export opportunities if applicable, and proprietary protection in the form of patents. This market prefers manufacturing and technology companies.

ESOPs

Successful ESOP conversions have an annual payroll of $250,000 to $300,000, a minimum 10 percent earnings, at least 15 employees, a high level of commitment to the company from owners and employees, and an equitable system of rewarding employees. ESOPs are a good strategy for service or manufacturing companies.

Warrants

This financing source usually is activated only when the price of the company's stock is rising, or its perceived value is going up due to increased sales, market domination, or asset acquisition. Reflecting the trends of the public market as a whole, warrant investors prefer manufacturing and technology companies.

F&Fs

This is the cheapest source of equity or debt capital available. Investor requirements are variable, but usually not as stringent as the requirements of outside investors or lenders. They look for enough cash flow to pay back the loan or pay small returns on the investment.

Exempt Offerings

Investor requirements are similar to IPO requirements, but with slightly more latitude in underlying assets and growth potential; revenue of $10 million+ preferred, earnings in the 5 to 10 percent range; proprietary protection (patents); market niche and a growing industry.

Convertibles

This market wants the cash flow and collateral strength needed to get a bank loan, as well as the growth potential of an equity investment: $10 million in annual revenues, earnings of 5 to 10 percent, solid financial assumptions underlying the projections, relatively low risk level, no existing debt, proprietary protection, and some growth potential.

Commercial Bank Loans

Lenders prefer primary, secondary and tertiary levels of collateral or assets, annual revenues of $5 million or more, rising earnings that conform to industry standards, safe competitive conditions, a solid management team with a track record, and no existing debt, proprietary protection.

LBOs

These lenders want traditional borrowing strength (see commercial bank loan above), with an emphasis on salable assets and continued cash flow to pay off the loan.

Finance Companies

Asset-based lending requires strong and continuing cash flow similar to commercial bank lending criteria, plus unusually strong assets against which to make the short-term loan. If debt repayment slows or stops, these lenders liquidate assets for which they hold title almost immediately.

Venture Capital

These investors want everything: the capacity to grow to $50 million in annual revenue in 5 to 10 years; 30 to 35 percent compounded annual returns; a leadership position in an emerging, global industry; broad and deep management credentials; and the potential to exit profitably in three to five years.

Joint Venture/Licensing/Tech Transfer Agreements

Like most corporate investors, this market isn't as concerned about such criteria as current cash flow or asset base as lenders are. It wants growth potential in a new industry, few or no competitors, and a complementary fit to specific needs for a product or local jobs, for example. Technology transfer investors look for proprietary protection in the form of patents, copyrights, and trademarks, in the United States and in global markets.

Partnerships

Partnership requirements are as diverse as the companies that create them, generally based on complementary management styles and credentials, market demands, products, technologies, or vertical integration. These investors tend to apply equity criteria, including growth potential in the same or a related industry, a benign competitive environment with little regulatory interference, proprietary protection, and enough staying power to sustain contract performance.

Mergers/Buyouts

Every company can be a potential merger or buyout when complementary operations and results are measured. In general, buyers want to maintain current operations with strong earnings plus acquire opportunities for growth: revenue and earnings continuity; a marketplace that is free from too many competitors or regulatory conditions; at least some growth potential in a thriving industry; and a smooth transition to their management.

Offshore Merchant Banks

Traditional U.S. borrowing criteria apply here, with a few additions: the company's ability to create jobs for the local economy, its ability to cover the cost of local environmental impact projects, and its long-term commitment to the contract.

Offshore Private Markets

These investors have requirements similar to the requirements of U.S. investors in IPOs. They also want a knowledge of offshore markets and trading trends; high growth potential in an emerging, global industry; and a long, reliable track record in the industry.

Offshore Corporations

Most corporations form alliances with U.S. companies in order to accomplish one specific purpose, such as, to distribute, manufacture, or combine product lines, rather than for a long-term trading relationship. They require that you be an expert in your field, that the company have the financial strength to perform its part of the contract, and that they have at least the potential to buy some or all rights to the product in the future.

U.S. Government

For capital from procurement and R&D programs, the company is expected only to deliver the product or service as specified in the bidding contract, and to have the technical expertise to complete the R&D project. Other lending and debt/equity programs require traditional borrowing strength plus collateral worth three times the value of the loan, as well as growth potential in the industry.

ESTIMATING COST

Now estimate the cost in time and money of the financing you want to do.

Public Market

IPO	One year; 40 percent of net proceeds
ESOP	One year; 30 percent of net proceeds
Warrants	Three months; 25 percent of net proceeds

Individuals

F&F	One month; $1,000–$2,000
Exempt offerings	Six months to one year; 35 percent of net proceeds
Convertibles	Six months to one year; 35 percent of net proceeds

Lenders

Commercial bank loans	Three to six months; prime rate plus 2–3 percent
LBOs	Three to six months; prime rate plus 2 percent
Finance companies	Three months; prime rate plus 5–6 percent per month

Corporations

Venture capital	Three to six months, variable; 30–60 percent equity giveup
Joint ventures/licensing/ transfer agreements	Six months; 15 percent of net tech. proceeds plus variable equity giveup, if applicable
Partnerships	Six months; 20 percent of net proceeds
Mergers/buyouts	Six months: controlling share of equity

Offshore

Merchant banks	Six months; prime or international rate plus variable percentage points
Private market	One year; 40 percent of net proceeds
Corporations	One year; 30–40 percent of net proceeds

Last, apply an inflationary/recessionary yardstick to the capital sources you have selected, based on the recent movement of interest rates, the change in global competition in your industry, and the outlook for the local/national economy. In general, equity sources are better during inflationary markets because stock prices and company valuations go up; debt sources are better during recessionary markets because interest rates go down.

Appropriate Capital-Raising Strategies When Market Movements Are Inflationary

- IPOs
- ESOPs
- Warrants
- Convertible securities with large equity feature
- Exempt offerings
- F&F
- Mergers/buyouts
- Partnerships
- Joint venture/licensing/technology transfer agreements
- Offshore private offerings

Appropriate Capital-Raising Strategies When Market Movements Are Recessionary

- Commercial bank loans
- Asset-based loans
- Lines of credit
- Federal and state government programs that emphasize lending
- LBOs
- Offshore merchant banks

Now contact one of the Business Service Centers listed in the Appendix if you need help in accessing any U.S. government financing, contractual, research, or procurement program.

Firms that specialize in research and development partnerships include:

- Daleco Research and
  Development, Inc.
  3388 Via Lido
  Newport Beach, CA 92663
  (800) 432-5326
- E.F. Hutton
  1 Battery Park Plaza
  New York, NY 10004
  (212) 747-8000
- Merrill Lynch Hubbard
  2 Broadway, 2nd Floor
  New York, NY 10004
  (212) 908-8409

- Paine Webber
  1285 Avenue of the Americas
  New York, NY 10020
  (212) 730-5826
- Prudential-Bache
  100 Gold Street
  New York, NY 10292
  (212) 791-1000
- Technology Funding, Inc.
  2000 Alameda De Las Pulgas
  San Mateo, CA 94403
  (415) 345-2200
- The Windsor Corporation
  120 West Grand Ave.
  Escondido, CA 92025
  (800) 821-4715

Please note that this is not a complete listing, but a representative example.

INDUSTRY/FINANCE ASSOCIATIONS IN THE PRIVATE SECTOR

The vast majority of trade and entrepreneurial associations are composed of small business owners who are by nature problem-solvers. Many groups were formed as competitors in an industry or service sector organized to work out common problems.

The following is a source list from which to get background and educational material for your financing package; referrals for local practitioners; and raw data on your industry including industry standards, financing and investment trends, and national statistics:

- American Bankers Association
  1120 Connecticut Ave., NW
  Washington, DC 20036
  (202) 467-4000
- American Farm Bureau Federation
  225 W. Touhy Ave.
  Park Ridge, IL 60068
  (312) 399-5700
- American Council of Life Insurance
  1850 K St., NW—Suite 600
  Washington, DC 20006-2284
  (202) 862-4000

- American Entrepreneurs Association
  2311 Pontius Ave.
  Los Angeles, CA 90064
  (213) 478-0437
  Sells 250 start-up business manuals;
  free counseling and monthly
  magazine to members
- American Financial Services
  Association
  1101 14th St., NW
  Washington, DC 20005
  (202) 289-0400

- American Health Care Association
  1200 15th St., NW
  Washington, DC 20005
  (202) 833-2050
- American Hotel and Motel
  Association
  888 7th Ave.
  New York, NY 10106
  (212) 265-4506
- American Insurance Association
  85 John St.
  New York, NY 10038
  (212) 669-0400
- American Petroleum Institute
  1220 L St., NW
  Washington, DC 20005
  (202) 682-8000
- American Retail Federation
  1616 H St., NW
  Washington, DC 20006
  (202) 783-7971
- American Society of Travel Agents
  4400 MacArthur Blvd., NW
  Washington, DC 20007
  (202) 965-7520
- American Trucking Association
  2200 Mill Road
  Alexandria, VA 22314
  (703) 838-1800
- Appraisers Association of America
  60 East 42nd St.
  New York, NY 10165
  (212) 867-9775
  Source for industry standards and
  local valuation referrals
- Associated Builders and Contractors
  729 15th St., NW
  Washington, DC 20005
  (202) 637-8800
- Association of Data Processing
  Service Organizations
  1300 N. 17th St.—Suite 300
  Arlington, VA 22209
  (703) 522-5055
- Chamber of Commerce of the U.S.
  1615 H St., NW
  Washington, DC 20062
  (202) 659-6000
  Among other functions, provides
  data, opinion and analysis direct to

small business owners; call
301/468-5128 to get U.S. Chamber
Staff Specialists.

- Computer & Business Equipment
  Manufacturers Association
  311 First St., NW—Suite 500
  Washington, DC 20001
  (202) 737-8888
- Consulting Engineers Council
  1401 17th Street—Suite 400
  Denver, CO 80202
  (303) 292-5722
  Source for data/statistics about
  engineering practice in the service
  sector
- Electronic Industries Association
  2001 Eye St., NW
  Washington, DC 20006
  (202) 457-4900
- Health Industry Distributors
  Association
  1701 Pennsylvania Ave., NW
  Washington, DC 20006
  (202) 857-1166
- Independent Bankers Association
  of America
  1625 Massachusetts Ave., NW
  Washington, DC 20036
  (202) 332-8980
  Source for banks that specialize in
  small deals
- Information Industry Association
  316 Pennsylvania Ave., SE
  Washington, DC 20003
  (202) 544-1969
- International Association for
  Financial Planning
  5775 Peachtree Dunwoody Road,
  NE—#120-C
  Atlanta, GA 30342
  (404) 395-1605
  Source for local financial planner
  referrals and data about the financial
  planning service sector
- International Franchise Association
  1025 Connecticut Ave., NW
  Washington, DC 20036
  (202) 659-0790
  Source for industry standards and
  local referrals

- International Reciprocal
  Trade Association
  1011 North Vail Street
  Alexandria, VA 22304
  (703) 578-3845
  Source for global barter statistics and
  trends, local referrals
- Investor Responsibility
  Research Center
  1319 F Street, NW
  Washington, DC 20004
  (202) 833-3727
  Source for data on the impact of
  ethical investment issues on small
  companies.
- National Association of
  Development Companies
  1612 K St., NW—Suite 706
  Washington, DC 20006
  (202) 785-8484
  Offers training and technical
  assistance, and an annual
  membership conference;
  SBA/Congressional liaison
- National Association of
  Investors Corporation
  1515 East 11 Mile Road
  Royal Oak, MI 48067
  (313) 543-0612
  Source for local referrals on
  investment clubs
- National Association of
  Manufacturers
  1776 F St., NW
  Washington, DC 20006
  (202) 637-3046
  Primary data source for the
  manufacturing industries
- National Association of Realtors
  430 North Michigan Ave.
  Chicago, IL 60611
  (312) 329-8000
  Source for industry information
- National Association of Small
  Business Investment Companies
  1156 15th St., NW—Suite 1101
  Washington, DC 20005
  (202) 833-8230
  Source for local referrals and
  application standards; sells SBIC and
  MESBIC directories; capital-raising
  reference material

- National Association of Women
  Business Owners
  221 N. La Salle St.—Suite 2026
  Chicago, IL 60601
  (312) 346-2330
  Provides local counseling and
  networking; monthly programs;
  annual national conference
- National Business Incubation
  Association
  P.O. Box 882
  Fairfax, VA 22030-0882
  (703) 765-0927
  Source for incubator industry
  statistics and local referrals
- National Federation of
  Independent Business
  600 Maryland Ave., SW—Suite 700
  Washington, DC—20024
  (202) 554-9000
  Provides data on economic trends,
  small business studies,
  entrepreneurship educational
  materials; lobbies for small business;
  holds regional conferences.
- National Small Business Association
  1604 K St., NW
  Washington, DC 20006
  (202) 293-8830
  Provides "Bidder's Early Alert
  Message" system for Federal
  contracting opportunities, and
  monthly small business newsletter.
- National Venture Capital Association
  1655 North Fort Meyer Drive
  Arlington, VA 22209
  (202) 528-4370
  Source for local referrals and industry
  statistics
- Printing Industries of America
  1730 N. Lynn St.
  Arlington, VA 22209
  (703) 841-8100
- Small Business High Technology
  Institute
  3300 No. Central Avenue
  Phoenix, AZ 85012
  (602) 277-6603
  Source for high-technology data in
  selected industries, local referrals

- Small Business United
  69 Hickory Drive
  Waltham, MA 02154
  (617) 890-9070
  Provides management assistance,
  educational programs,
  troubleshooting and counseling,
  regional networking data, and
  regional small business promotion.
- Technology Transfer Society
  611 North Capitol Avenue
  Indianapolis, IN 46204
  (317) 262-5022
  Source for worldwide technology
  transfer flow trends, local referrals

- Venture Economics
  Wellesley, MA
  Source for venture capital industry
  data
- Western Association of Venture
  Capitalists
  3000 Sand Hill Road
  Building 2, Suite 260
  Menlo Park, CA 94025
  Source for venture capital industry
  activity on the West Coast.

STATE GOVERNMENT FINANCING PROGRAMS FOR SMALL BUSINESS

All 50 states offer a wide variety of programs that help small companies raise debt or equity capital. The state can participate in a private-sector partnership, an incubator, for example, or it can partner with a municipality or federal government agency to provide a variety of financing mechanisms. State governments also create new financial instruments that respond to local requirements. Because state government participation is flexible, it can be confusing to identify all the programs, financing mechanisms, and resources available in your state. The best way to see what is available by state is to contact the National Council of State Legislatures, which tracks business development programs by industry and by state.

- National Council of State Legislatures
  1125 Seventeenth Street
  Denver, CO 80202
  (303) 292-6600

The following is a sampling of small-business financing and business development programs available, by state:

- Alabama
  Alabama Development Office
  State Capitol
  Montgomery, AL 36130
  (205) 263-0048
  Offers financing assistance in the
  form of a business loan program and

  venture capital; a small-business
  procurement program;
  minority/women opportunities in the
  form of business loans, venture
  capital procurement help, set-asides,
  managerial or technical help, and tax
  incentives. A portion of the state's

investment portfolio is deposited with Alabama banks or S&Ls to be linked to individuals loans made to eligible small businesses or farmers.

- Alaska
Office of Enterprise, Department of
  Commerce
Pouch D
Juneau, AK 99811
(907) 465-2018
Offers financing help in the form of business loans, demographic data, managerial/technical help, advocacy, and procurement assistance. The Alaskan Industrial Development cap was raised to $5 million to provide for small business development loans.

- Arizona
Office of Business and Trade, Dept.
  of Commerce
1700 West Washington Street, 4th
  floor
Phoenix, AZ 85007
(602) 255-5374
Offers managerial/technical help, training, demographic data, and procurement assistance and set-asides.

- Arkansas
Small Business Development Center
University of Arkansas
Library Building, Room 512
33rd and University
Little Rock, AR 72204
(501) 371-5381
Offers financial assistance in the form of a business loan program, advocacy, managerial/technical assistance, demographic data and an Enterprise Zone. The Arkansas Development Finance Authority is required to coordinate economic development in rural areas.

- California
Office of Small Business
  Development
Department of Commerce
1121 L Street—Suite 600
Sacramento, CA 95814
(916) 445-6545
Offers financial assistance in the form of business loans, venture capital, and

tax incentives; procurement help and set-asides; an Enterprise Zone; demographic data; managerial/technical assistance; and advocacy. State procurement participation goals were set for minority enterprises at 15% and for women-owned firms at 5%, which applies to manufacturing and service companies.

- Colorado
Business Information Center
Office of Regulatory Reform
1525 Sherman St.—Room 110
Denver, CO 80203
(303) 866-3933
Offers financial assistance in the form of business loans, small-business procurement, advocacy, and demographic data. The state created a Small Business Development Credit Corporation, which is state-regulated and privately-funded as a nonbank lending institution to provide financing and management assistance to small businesses.

- Connecticut
Small Business Services
Department of Economic
  Development
210 Washington St.
Hartford, CT 06106
(203) 566-4051
Offers financial assistance in the form of business loans, ven- ture capital and tax incentives; advocacy; managerial/technical assistance; demographic data, an Enterprise Zone; and training. The Financial Capital Act consolidated all loan programs and funding sources under one department and streamlined the process of applying for financial assistance.

- Delaware
Economic Development Office
99 King's Highway, P.O. Box 1401
Dover, DE 19903
(302) 736-4271
Offers financial assistance in the form of tax incentives and initiatives; advocacy; demographic daata; training; and an Enterprise Zone. The

Delaware Technical Innovation program promotes the development and utilization of technology by the small business sector.

- District of Columbia
  Office of Business and Economic
     Development
  District Building—Room 208
  1350 Pennsylvania Ave., NW
  Washington, DC 20004
  (202) 727-6600
  Offers financial assistance in the form of business loans and venture capital; minority/women procurement and set-asides; advocacy; managerial/technical assistance; and demographic data. The Local Small Business Procurement Act designates specified purchases as small business set-asides. Only small, local firms may bid on these purchases.

- Florida
  Small Business Development Center
  University of West Florida, Building 8
  Pensacola, FL 32514
  (904) 474-2908
  Offers financial assistance in the form of venture capital; advocacy; demographic data; an Enterprise Zone, managerial/technical assistance; and small-business procurement and set-asides. A 1988 Economic Development Act creates the position of Export Finance Officer to help the development of international exports by small- and medium-sized firms.

- Georgia
  Small Business Development Center
  1180 East Broad St.—Chicopee
     Complex
  Athens, GA 30602
  (404) 542-1721
  Offers financial assistance in the form of tax incentives and initiatives; training; advocacy; demographic data; managerial/technical assistance; and procurement and set-aside programs. The state created a Small Minority Business Development Corporation to provide support for firms

with annual gross sales of $6 million or less, 51 percent minority control, and fewer than 300 employees.

- Hawaii
  Small Business Information Service
  250 South King St.—Room 724
  Honolulu, HI 96813
  (808) 548-7645
  Offers financial assistance in the form of business loans and venture capital; minority/women programs including business loans, venture capital, procurement help, and set-asides; advocacy; managerial/technical assistance; demographic data; an Enterprise Zone; and small business procurement and set-asides. A one-stop office was created to handle the application and registration processes for businesses that need permits.

- Idaho
  Division of Economic and
     Community Affairs,
  Department of Commerce
  State Capitol—Room 108
  Boise, ID 83720
  (208) 334-2470
  Offers financial assistance in the form of business loans; procurement assistance; minority/women procurement programs; demographic data; training; managerial/technical assistance; and advocacy.

- Illinois
  Bureau of Small Business,
     Department of Commerce and
     Community Affairs
  620 Adams St.
  Springfield, IL 62701
  (217) 785-7500
  Offers financial assistance in the form of business loans, venture capital, and tax incentives; minority/women business loans; procurement programs; an Enterprise Zone; demographic data; managerial/technical assistance; and advocacy.

- Indiana
  Division of Business Expansion,
     Department of Commerce
  Indiana Commerce Center

1 North Capital Ave.—Suite 700
Indianapolis, IN 46204
(317) 232-8800
Offers financial assistance in the
form of business loans, venture
capital and tax incentives; minority/
women programs; procurement
programs; an Enterprise Zone; demographic data; managerial/technical
assistance; and advocacy. An Export
Finance Authority was created to
raise money through the Indiana Employment Development Commission
and make it available, in tandem with
banks, to small- and medium-sized
firms.

- Iowa
Small Business Division, Iowa
    Development Commission
600 East Court Ave.—Suite A
Des Moines, IA 50309
(515-281-8310
Offers financial assistance in the
form of business loans and venture
capital; minority/women programs;
procurement programs; managerial/
technical assistance; and advocacy.
An economic development corporation was created to help rural small
business financing. It is financed by
the sale of memberships to financial
institutions, $2 million in state lot-
tery profits, and stock sales. A low-
interest loan program helps Iowa
communities with decaying and out-
dated infrastructures to retain and attract new firms and industry through
public works projects. Half of the
money is earmarked for communities
with a population of under 5,000.
Funding is generated by bonds
backed by $4 million in state lottery
profits.

- Kansas
Small Business Development Center
Wichita State University
021 Clinton Hall—Box 48
Wichita, KS 67208
(316) 689-3193
Offers financial assistance in the
form of business loans, venture
capital, and tax incentives; minority/

women programs; procurement
assistance; demographic data; an Enterprise Zone; managerial/technical
assistance; and advocacy. Legislation
exempted new farming and manufacturing equipment from the state sales
tax for one year. Investment tax
credits in Kansas Venture Capital
Inc., certified venture capital companies, and certified seed capital pools
may be claimed in one year instead
of four to increase the availability of
capital for small and startup
businesses.

- Kentucky
Business Information Clearinghouse
Commerce Cabinet
Capitol Plaza Tower—22nd floor
Frankfort, KY 40601
(502) 564-4252
Offers financial assistance in the
form of business loans, venture
capital, and tax incentives; minority/
women programs; procurement
programs; advocacy; managerial/
technical assistance; training; demographic data; and an Enterprise Zone.
The Kentucky Development Finance
Authority makes working capital
loans to assist mining, health care,
and agricultural production.

- Louisiana
Small Business Specialist
Office of Commerce and Industry
1 Maritime Plaza, P.O. Box 94185
Baton Rouge, LA 70802-9185
(504) 342-9224
Offers financial assistance in the
form of business loans, venture
capital, and tax incentives; minority/
women financing; procurement
programs for small business; an
Enterprise Zone, demographic data;
training; managerial/technical assistance; and advocacy. All goods and
services bought in the construction
of roads or highways are subject to a
minimum 10 percent set-aside for
socially or economically disadvantaged individuals and women-owned
businesses.

- Maine
Small Business Development Center
University of Southern Maine
246 Deering Ave.
Portland, ME 04102
(207) 780-4420
Offers financial assistance in the
form of business loans and tax
incentives; procurement programs;
demographic data; training; manage-
rial/technical assistance; and
advocacy.
    Legislation removed the ceiling
on statutory loan guarantees for the
Finance Authority's Small Business
Mortgage Insurance Program.

- Massachusetts
Small Business Assistance Division
Department of Commerce
100 Cambridge St.—13th floor
Boston, MA 02202
Offers financial assistance in the
form of business loans, venture
capital, and tax incentives; minority/
women programs; procurement
programs; an Enterprise Zone,
demographic data; training; and
managerial/technical assistance. A
new Universal Health Care bill requires employers to provide health insurance for qualified full- and
part-time employees as of 1992. Self-
employed, employers with five or
fewer workers, seasonal or agricultural employees, new businesses,
and existing health plan enrollees
are exempt.

- Michigan
Local Development Service
Department of Commerce
P.O. Box 30225
Lansing, MI 48909
(517) 373-3530
Offers financial assistance in the
form of business loans and tax incentives; procurement programs; minor-
ity/women programs; demographic
data; training; managerial/technical
assistance; and advocacy. A new program sets a minimum state contracting goal of 3% for purchases of goods,
services, and construction, from

which between $5 and $7 million
handicapped-owned contract awards
are expected to result.

- Minnesota
Small Business Assistance Office
Department of Energy and
    Economic Development
900 American Center
150 E. Kellogg Blvd.
St. Paul, MN 55107
(612) 296-3871
Offers financial assistance in the
form of business loans, venture
capital, and tax incentives; minority/
women programs; procurement
programs; and an Enterprise Zone;
demographic data; training;
managerial/technical assistance;
and advocacy.

- Mississippi
Small Business Clearinghouse,
    Research and Development Center
3825 Ridgewood Rd.
Jackson, MS 39211-6453
(601) 982-6231
Offers financial assistance in the
form of business loans; minority/
women set-asides; procurement
programs; an Enterprise Zone; demographic data; training; managerial/
technical assistance; and advocacy. A
Small Enterprise Development Finance Act provides long-term, fixed-
rate capital to small businesses in
rural areas. Local banks will issue let-
ters of credit, which will allow many
smaller banks to participate in state
economic development programs.

- Missouri
Small Business Development Office
    Division of Community and
    Economic Developpment
P.O. Box 118
Jefferson City, MO 65102
(314) 751-4982
Offers financial assistance in the
form of business loans, venture
capital, and tax incentives; minority/
women programs; an Enterprise
Zone; demographic data; training;
managerial/technical assistance. The
Major Industry Fund and linked-

deposit program (MOBUCKS) were enlarged so that expanding small firms that add jobs above the previous loan-qualifying limit of 10 employees can be eligible for funds at 3 percent below the Treasury bill rate.

- Montana
  Business Assistance Division
  Department of Commerce
  1424 Ninth Ave.
  Helena, MT 59620
  (406) 444-3923
  Offers financial assistance in the form of business loans, venture capital, and tax incentives; procurement programs; minority/women programs; demographic data; training; managerial/technical assistance; and advocacy.

- Nebraska
  Small Business Division
  Department of Economic
    Development
  P.O. Box 94666, 301 Centennial
    Mall South
  Lincoln, NE 68509
  (402) 471-3111
  Offers financial assistance in the form of business loans and tax incentives; procurement assistance; demographic data; training; managerial/technical assistance; and advocacy. A Prompt Payment Act was enacted directing state government entities to be timely in their payments to private suppliers.

- Nevada
  Small Business Development Center
  University of Nevada/College of
    Business Administration
  Business Building—Room 411
  Reno, NV 89557-0016
  Offers financial assistance in the form of business loans; minority/women programs; procurement assistance; demographic data; training; and managerial/technical assistance.

- New Hampshire
  Industrial Development Authority
  4 Park St.—Room 302
  Concord, NH 03301
  (603) 271-2391

Offers financial assistance in the form of business loans; minority/women programs; procurement programs; demographic data; training; managerial/technical assistance. The business profits tax was changed so that a loss may be carried forward.

- New Jersey
  Office of Small Business Assistance
  Department of Commerce and
    Economic Development
  1 West State St.—CN 823
  Trenton, NJ 08625
  (609) 984-4442
  Offers financial assistance in the form of business loans and tax incentives; minority/women programs; procurement programs; an Enterprise Zone; demographic data; training; managerial/technical assistance; and advocacy.

- New Mexico
  Business Development and
    Expansion
  Department of Economic
    Development and Tourism
  Bataan Memorial Building
  Suite 201
  Santa Fe, NM 87503
  (505) 827-6204
  Offers financial assistance in the form of business loans, venture capital, and tax incentives; minority/women programs; procurement programs; demographic data; training; managerial/technical assistance; and advocacy. Local qualifying communities may self-designate as Free Enterprise Zones, offering tax enhyancements to businesses locating in the zones.

- New York
  Small Business Division, New York
  Department of Commerce
  230 Park Ave.—Room 834
  New York, NY 10169
  (212) 309-0400
  Offers financial assistance in the form of business loans and venture capital; minority/women programs; procurement programs; demographic

data; tax incentives; training; managerial/technical assistance; and advocacy. The corporate franchise tax decreased from 10 to 8 percent, saving 50,000 small businesses about $61 million annually.

- North Carolina
  Small Business Development
    Division
  Department of Commerce
  Dobbs Building—Room 282
  Salisbury St.
  Raleigh, NC 27611
  (919) 733-6254
  Offers financial assistance in the form of business loans; minority/women procurement programs; procurement programs; an Enterprise Zone; demographic data; training; managerial/technical assistance; and advocacy.

- North Dakota
  Small Business Specialist
  Economic Development Commission
  Liberty Memorial Building
  Bismarck, ND 58505
  (701) 224-2810
  Offers financial assistance in the form of business loans, venture capital, and tax incentives; procurement assistance; demographic data; training; managerial/technical assistance; and advocacy. The Center for Technology Transfer provides a mainframe computer available to small engineering and architectural firms.

- Ohio
  Small Business Office
  Ohio Department of Development
  P.O. Box 1001
  Columbus, OH 43266-0101
  (614) 466-4945
  Offers financial assistance in the form of business loans and tax incentives; minority/women programs; procurement help; and business development programs.

- Oklahoma
  Small Business Development Center
  Station A—517 West University

Durant, OK 74701
(405) 924-0277
Offers minority/women programs; procurement programs; and business development programs. Linked-deposit legislation provides incentives for banks holding state funds to make capital available to small businesses, with interest rates at the two-year T-bill level and a maximum markup of 5.5 percent.

- Oregon
  Oregon Economic Development
    Department
  595 Cottage St., NE
  Salem, OR 97310
  (503) 373-1200
  Offers financial assistance in the form of business loans, venture capital, and tax incentives; minority/women programs; and business development programs.

- Pennsylvania
  Small Business Action Center
  Department of Commerce
  483 Forum Building
  Harrisburg, PA 17120
  (717) 783-5700
  Offers financial assistance in the form of business loans and venture capital; minority/women programs; procurement programs; and business development programs.

- Rhode Island
  Small Business Development
    Division
  Department of Economic
    Development
  7 Jackson Walkway
  Providence, RI 02903
  (401) 277-2601
  Offers financial assistance in the form of business loans and tax incentives; minority/women programs; procurement programs; and business development. The Department of Economic Development was appropriated $123,000 to develop an export assistance center that helps small firms identify markets and provide counseling on export

documentation, logistics, financing, and training issues.

- South Carolina
  Business Assistance Services and
  Information Center
  Industry-Business and Community
  Services Division
  State Development Board
  P.O. Box 927
  Columbia, SC 29202
  (803) 758-3046
  Offers financial assistance in the form of business loans and tax incentives; minority/women programs; procurement pro- grams; and business development. A $10 million seed capital fund was established to promote small business development.

- South Dakota
  Small Business Development Center
  University of South Dakota
  414 East Clark St.
  Vermillion, SC 57069-2390
  (605) 677-5272
  Offers procurement assistance and business development programs.

- Tennessee
  Small Business Office,
  Department of Economic and
  Community Development
  320 6th Ave. North—7th floor
  Nashville, TN 37219
  (615) 741-2626
  Offers minority/women programs, procurement assistance; and business development.

- Texas
  Small and Minority Business
  Assistance Division
  Economic Development Commission
  P.O. Box 12728 Capitol Station—410
  East 5th St.
  Austin, TX 78711
  (512) 472-5059
  Offers financial assistance in the form of business loans; minority/women programs; procurement assistance; and business development programs.

- Utah
  Small Business Development Center
  University of Utah
  Business Classroom Building—Room
  410-BUC
  Salt Lake City, UT 84112
  (801) 581-7905
  Offers financial assistance in the form of business loans and venture capital; venture capital for minority/women firms; procurement programs; and business development programs. City and county governments were authorized by the legislature to allow private firms to operate correctional facilities.

- Vermont
  Small Business Development Center
  University of Vermont Extension
  Service
  Morrill Hall, Burlington, VT 05405
  (802) 656-2990
  Offers financial assistance in the form of business loans; minority/women programs; procurement programs; and business development programs.

- Virginia
  Small Business Coordinator
  Department of Economic
  Development
  1000 Washington Building
  Richmond, VA 23219
  (804) 786-3791
  Offers financial assistance in the form of business loans; minority/women programs; and business development programs.

- Washington
  Small Business Development Center
  441 Todd Hall, Washington State
  University
  Pullman, WA 99164
  (509) 335-1576
  Offers financial assistance in the form of business loans, venture capital, and tax incentives; minority/women programs; procurement assistance; and business development. The legislature directed the Department of Trade and Economic Development

to establish "Washington Market-place," an import replacement program resulting in community-based economic development. The voluntary program matches buyers with nearby suppliers through a competitive and confidential bidding process.

- West Virginia
Small Business Division
Governor's Office of Community and
   Industrial Development
Capitol Complex
Charleston, WV 25305
(304) 348-2960
Offers financial assistance in the form of business loans and tax incentives; minority/women programs; procurement programs; and business development.

- Wisconsin
Small Business Ombudsman
Department of Development
123 W. Washington Ave.
Madison, WI 53707
(608) 266-0562
Offers financial assistance in the form of business loans and tax incentives; minority/women programs; procurement assistance; and business development. A special program called "1-800-HELP-BUSiness" has been created.

- Wyoming
Economic Development Division
Economic Developpment and
   Stabilization Board
Herschler Building—3rd Floor East
Cheyenne, WY 82002
(307) 777-7287
Offers financial assistance in the form of business loans; procurement set-asides; and business development. The Community Development Authority has chartered a subsidiary corporation to manage and originate economic development loans. The legislature provided an additional $50 million for low-interest business loans through Wyoming banks.

RESOURCE LIST FOR THE TOP 25 INTERNATIONAL MARKETS, BY CONTINENT

Asia

- China
Preparatory Office of Shanghai World
   Trade Center
c/o CCPIT Shanghai Sub-Council
33 Zhong Shan Dong Yi Lu
Shanghai, PRC
Telephone: 232348
Telex: 33290 SCPIT CN

- Hong Kong
World Trade Centre Hong Kong
c/o World Trade Centre Club
   Hong Kong
2/M & 3/F World Trade Centre
Causeway Bay, Hong Kong
Telephone: 5-779528
Telex: 71729 WTCEN HX

- India
Trade Development Authority
Bank of Baroda Building
16, Sansad Marg
P.O. Box 767
New Delhi 110001, India
Telephone: 312819   Telex: 2735

- Japan
JETRO (Japanese External
   Trade Organization)
2-5 Toranomon, 2-chome
Minato-Ku, Tokyo, Japan

- Singapore
Singapore Economic Development
   Board
1 Maritime Square, No. 10-40
World Trade Centre (Lobby D),
   Singapore 0409
Telephone: 2710844   Telex: 26233

- South Korea
World Trade Center Korea
Korean Traders Association
10-1, 2-Ka Hoehyon-Dong,
   Chung-Ku
C.P.O. Box 1117, Seoul, Korea
Telephone: 771-41   Telex: K24265

- Taiwan
Taipei World Trade Center Co., Ltd.
Sung Shan Airport Terminal

340 Tun Hwa North Road
Taipei, Taiwan
Telephone: (02) 715-1551
Telex: 28094 TPEWTC

Australia

- Department of Trade
Stockland House
181 Castlereagh Street
Sydney, N.S.W. 2000

Europe

- Britain
World Trade Centre London
International House
Saint Katharine's Way
London, E1 9UN,
   United Kingdom
Telephone: 01-488-2400
Telex: 884671

- France
Comite Parisien de Congres
24 Avenue de l'Opera, 75001 Paris
Telephone: 296-03-61
Telex: 210 311F

- Italy
World Trade Center Italy SRL
Palazzo WTC
Centro Direzionale Milanofiori
20090 Assago (Milan), Italy
Telephone: (02) 824-4086

- The Netherlands
Ministry of Economic Affairs
P.O. Box 20101, 2500 EC
The Hague, The Netherlands
Telephone: 070-798911

- Switzerland
Swiss Office for the Development
   of Trade
Avant-Poste Ch-1001
Lausanne, Switzerland
Telephone: 021-20-3231

- West Germany
German Foreign Trade Information
   Office
P.O.B. 108007, Blaubach 13
D-5000 Cologne 1, West Germany
Telephone: (221)-20571

Middle East and Africa

- Saudi Arabia
Jeddah World Trade Center (R-IP)
Saudi Economic & Development Co.
   Ltd. (SEDCO)
P.O. Box 4384
Jeddah, Saudi Arabia
Telephone: (02) 644-0920-1
Telex: 400197 SEDCO SJ

- Ivory Coast
Department of Foreign Trades
Abidjan, Ivory Coast
Telephone: 322627

- Nigeria
World Trade Center of Nigeria, Ltd.
Western House, 8th Floor
8/10 Broad Street, P.O. Box 4466
Lagos, Nigeria
Telephone: 631499/632151

The Americas

- Canada
Department of Industry Trade &
   Commerce
235 Queen Street
Ottawa, Ontario, Canada KIA 0H5
Telephone: (613) 995-5771

- Mexico
World Trade Center de Mexico
Central de Comercio Mundial S.A.
Mariano Escobedo 491-494
Delegacion Miguel Hidalgo
C.P. 11570 Mexico City, Mexico
Telephone: 254-1659

- Argentina
American Chamber of Commerce
   in Argentina
Avenida R. Saenz Pena 567
1352 Buenos Aires, Argentina
Telephone: 33-5591

- Brazil
World Trade Center do Rio de
   Janeiro
Rua Mexico, 111/Gr. 1504-andaar
Rio de Janeiro, Brazil 20031
Telephone: (02) 2243065/2529524
Telex: 22239

- Chile
Chamber of Commerce of the USA
   in Chile

Huerfanos 669, Officina 608
P.O. Box 4131
Santiago, Chile
Telephone: 393163

- Colombia
Ministry of Economic Development
Carrera 13, No. 27-00
Apartado Aereo 3412
Bogota, Colombia
Telephone: 234-0540

- Venezuela
Venezuelan-American Chamber of
    Commerce & Industry
Apartado 5181
Caracas 1010, Venezuela
Telephone: (582) 283-8355

USSR

- World Trade Center Moscow
v/ov/o SOVINCENTR
12 Krasnopresnenskaya nab.
123610 Moscow, U.S.S.R.
Telephone: 2566303
Telex: 411486 SOVIN SU

FINANCE-RELATED SMALL BUSINESS PUBLICATIONS/ DATABASES

- Directory of Online Databases
    Cuadra Associates, Inc.
2001 Wilshire Blvd, Suite 305
Santa Monica, CA 90403
(213) 829-9972
Provides comprehensive listings of
available databases

- Federal Acquisition Regulations/U.S.
    Government
Purchasing and Sales Directory/
    Selling to the
Military/How to Sell to the U.S.
    Government: U.S. Government
    Printing Office
Washington, DC (202) 783-3238
Everything you need to know about
Federal procurement and sales pro-
grams ($90)

- Fintex International Economic
    Summaries
NewsNet
945 Haverford Road
Bryn Mawr, PA 19010

(800) 345-5220
Summaries of financial, economic,
and political news affecting international finance markets.

- Foreign Traders Index
U.S. Department of Commerce
Trade Facilitation Information
    Services Division
ITA/1033/FTI
Washington, DC
(202) 377-2988
Categorizes 150,000 foreign firms
that import U.S. goods or want to represent U.S. exporters, including manufacturers, wholesalers, retailers, and
sales agents. Provides data by firm according to SIC classification.

- High Technology Business
Infotechnology Publishing Corp.
320 Park Avenue
New York, NY 10022
(212) 891-7500
Monthly magazine specializing in
the activity and financings of high-
technology industries; non-technical.

- Inc.
P.O. Box 2542
Boulder, CO 80322
(800) 525-0643

- Inferential Focus
200 Madison Avenue
New York, NY 10016
(212) 683-2060
Private "futurist" consulting firm
specializing in economic and socio-
logical trends.

- International Financial Statistics
    (IFS)
International Monetary Fund Bureau
    of Statistics
700 19th Street NW
Washington, DC 20431
(202) 477-3243
Financial statistics from over 120
countries, including international
transactions (value, volume, prices
and capital), national accounts
(private, investment, and GNP),
population, and exchange rates. This
highly authoritative source is updated
monthly, and carries historical data
as far back as 1948.

- Mergers & Acquisitions
  229 S. 18th Street
  Rittenhouse Square
  Philadelphia, PA 19103
  (215) 875-2332
  Bimonthly magazine on national
  merger activity and trends.
- Omni Online Database Directory
  MacMillan Publishing Company
  866 Third Avenue
  New York, NY 10022
  Provides comprehensive listings of
  available databases.
- Venture
  521 Fifth Avenue
  New York, NY 10175
  (212) 682-7373

Monthly magazine for small-business
owners with an emphasis on small financing.
- U.S. Exports
  U.S. Census Bureau/Foreign Trade
    Division
  Washington, DC 20033
  (301) 763-7273
  Government and non-government
  statistics on exports from the U.S.
  to other nations. Searches available
  by type of commodity, dates, net
  quantities, net values, and country
  of destination.
- Success
  Hal Holdings Corporation
  342 Madison Avenue
  New York, NY 10173

U.S. GOVERNMENT FUNDING SOURCES

- U.S. Small Business Administration (SBA)
  1441 L Street, NW
  Washington, DC 20416
  (800) 368-5855 (Main number)
  (202) 653-6470 (Financial assistance)
  (202) 653-6508 (Procurement assistance)
  (202) 653-6330 (Business development)
  (202) 653-5688 (Minority business development)
  (202) 653-7794 (International trade assistance)
  Contract loans, business disaster assistance, export revolving line of credit,
  handicapped loans, physical disaster loans; SBICs, regular business loans,
  seasonal lines of credit, energy loans, disaster loans, economic opportunity
  loans, loan development companies, pollution control loans, and other special
  programs.
- Export-Import Bank of the United States (Eximbank)
  811 Vermont Ave. NW
  Washington, D.C. 20571
  (202) 566-8819
  Bulk agricultural commodity export insurance, FICA export credit insurance,
  medium term credit, small-business credit leasing, private export funding
  corporation, procurement, and export financing
- Overseas Private Investment Corporation (OPIC)
  1129 20th St. NW
  Washington, DC 20527
  (202) 653-2800
  Direct investment loans, foreign investment guarantees, pre-investment assistance, and various insurance plans
- Commodity Credit Corporation (CCC)
  Department of Agriculture

12th St. and Jefferson Dr., SW
Washington, DC 20250
(202) 447-4026

- (State) Departments of Commerce and Economic Development Councils
Commerce Productivity Center
U.S. Department of Commerce—Room 7413
Washington, DC 20230
(202) 377-0940
(see listing of programs by state in Chapter 4)

- Department of Commerce
14th Street between Constitution and E Sts, NW
Washington, DC 20230
(202) 377-2000
    Census Bureau: (202) 763-4100
    Bureau of Economic Analysis: (202) 523-0777
    Office of Productivity, Technology and Innovation: (202) 377-1984
    National Technical Information Service: (703) 487-4600
    Economic Development Administration: (202) 377-5113
    International Trade Administration: (202) 377-3808
    National Bureau of Standards: (202) 921-2318
    Minority Business Development Agency: (202) 377-1936

- Incubator Information Services
Office of Private Sector Initiatives/SBA
1441 L Street, NW—Room 317
Washington, DC 20416
(202) 653-7880

- Small Business Investment Research (SBIR) Program
(listed by department of project origination and funding):
Department of Agriculture: (202) 475-5022
Department of Commerce: (202) 377-1472
Department of Defense: (202) 697-9383
Department of Education: (202) 254-8247
Department of Energy: (202) 353-5867
Department of Interior: (202) 634-4704
Department of Health/Human Services: (202) 245-7300
Department of Transportation: (202) 494-2051
Environmental Protection Agency: (202) 382-7445
Nat'l Aeronautics and Space Adm.: (202) 453-8702
National Science Foundation: (202) 357-7527
Nuclear Regulatory Commission: (202) 427-4250

- U.S. International Development Cooperation Agency and Agency for
International Development (AID)
320 21st St., NW
Washington, DC 20523
(202) 632-9620
Small/disadvantaged business utilization and foreign trade opportunities

- General Services Administration
18th and F Sts., NW
Washington, DC 20405
(202) 566-1231
Provides Federal supply schedules and sells Federal surplus property

Appendix

PRIVATE-DEAL BROKERS

- U.S. Venture Development Corporation
  (private placements/$100,000 minimum size; $500,000 minimum IPO size)
  Washington, DC
  (202) 364-8890
- AIBC Investment Services, Inc.
  (private placements; prefers companies with less than $5 million in revenues)
  Miami, FL
  (305) 372-3646
- Meland Capital Corporation
  (private placements; prefers small local firms)
  St. Louis Park, MN
  (612) 541-1736
- M.W. Campbell & Co. Ltd.*
  (private placements; prefers small/start-up companies)
  Pittsburgh, PA
  (412) 441-9388
- Marketing Perspectives*
  (private placements; prefers minimum $250,000 in revenues/consumer-oriented companies)
  Dallas, TX
  (214) 661-1001

NATIONAL MARKET RESEARCH FIRMS

- DataPro Research
  1221 Avenue of the Americas
  New York, NY 10020
  (212) 512-3851
- Dataquest
  1290 Ridder Park Drive
  San Jose, CA 95131
  (408) 437-8000
- Freedonia Group
  2940 Noble Road
  Cleveland, OH 44121
  (216) 381-6100
- Frost & Sullivan
  106 Fulton Street
  New York, NY 10038
  (212) 233-1080
- International Data
  5 Speen Street
  Framingham, MA 01701
  (508) 872-8200
- International Resource Development
  21 Locust Avenue
  New Canaan, CT 06840
  (203) 866-7800
- Prognos
  1852 McCraren Road
  Highland Park, IL 60035
  (312) 831-136

* Merchant banking function available (The firm may invest its own capital in a deal.)

- Strategic Analysis
  Box 3485 R.D. 3
  Reading, PA 19606
  (215) 779-9080
- Technology Futures
  6034 W. Courtyard Drive
  Austin, TX 78730
  (512) 343-6468
- Venture Economics
  16 Laurel Avenue
  Wellesley Hills, MA 02181
  (617) 237-3111

BUSINESS SERVICE CENTERS

- District of Columbia and nearby
  Maryland and Virginia
  7th and D Sts., SW.—Room 1050
  Washington, DC 20407
  (202) 472-1293-1804
- Maine, Vermont, New Hampshire,
  Massachusetts, Connecticut,
  Rhode Island
  John W. McCormack Post Office and
  Courthouse
  Boston, MA 02109
  (617) 223-2868
- New York, New Jersey, Puerto Rico,
  Virgin Islands
  26 Federal Plaza
  New York, NY 10278
  (212) 264-1234
- Pennsylvania, Delaware, West
  Virginia, Maryland, Virginia
  9th and Market Sts.—Room 5142
  Philadelphia, PA 19107
  (215) 597-9613
- North Carolina, South Carolina,
  Georgia, Tennesee, Kentucky,
  Florida, Alabama, Mississippi
  Richard B. Russell Federal Building
  and Courthouse
  75 Spring Street
  Atlanta, GA 30303
  (404) 221-5103/3032
- Ohio, Indiana, Illinois, Michigan,
  Minnesota, Wisconsin
  230 South Dearborn St.
  Chicago, IL 60604
  (312) 353-5383

- Missouri, Iowa, Kansas, Nebraska
  1500 East Bannister Rd.
  Kansas City, MO 64131
  (816) 926-7203
- Arkansas, Louisiana, Texas,
  New Mexico, Oklahoma
  819 Taylor St.
  Fort Worth, TX 76102
  (817) 334-3284
- Gulf Coast from Brownsville, Texas,
  to New Orleans, Louisiana
  Federal Office Building and
  Courthouse
  515 Rusk St.
  Houston, TX 77002
  (713) 226-5787
- Colorado, North Dakota, South
  Dakota, Utah, Montana, Wyoming
  Building 41—Denver Federal Center
  Denver, CO 80225
  (303) 234-2216
- Northern California, Hawaii, all of
  Nevada except Clark County
  525 Market St.
  San Francisco, CA 94105
  (415) 556-0877/2122
- Los Angeles, Southern California,
  Arizona and Clark County, Nevada
  300 North Los Angeles St.
  Los Angeles, CA 90012
  (213) 688-3210
- Washington, Oregon, Idaho, Alaska
  440 Federal Building
  915 Second Ave.
  Seattle, WA 98174
  (206) 442-5556

NATIONAL RESEARCH REPORTS

- Newton-Evans Research
  3220 Corporate Court
  Ellicott City, MD 21043
  (301) 465-7316
  "Corporate Strategies in the U.S.
  Computer Industry, Vol I."
  Analyses of computer companies with
  more than $1 billion in revenue for
  1987.   ($395)

- Market Intelligence Research
  2525 Charleston Road
  Mountain View, CA 94043
  (415) 961-9000
  "Industrial Material Processing Laser
  Markets, Growth applications and
  Industries." Estimated $67.5 million
  1988 market to reach $85 million by
  1994.   ($995)
- Freedonia Group
  2940 Noble Road
  Cleveland, OH 44121
  (216) 381-6100
  "Antidioxants." U.S. antidioxant sales
  for the rubber, plastics, food, and
  lubricant industries to increase
  6.1% annually to $725 million by
  1992.   ($800)
- Input
  1280 Villa Street
  Mountain View, CA 94041
  (415) 961-3300
  "Federal Systems-Integration Market,
  1987–1992." Projects government
  demand for systems-integration and
  turnkey systems to be $4.8 billion by
  1992.   ($1,395)

NATIONAL AND INTERNATIONAL
U.S. ACCOUNTING FIRMS

- Altschuler, Melvoin and Glasser
  30 South Wacker Drive
  Chicago, IL 60606
  (312) 207-2800
- Arthur Andersen & Co.
  69 West Washington St.
  Chicago, IL 60602
  (312) 580-0069
- Baird, Kurtz & Dobson
  318 Park Central East
  Springfield, MO 65806
  (417) 865-8701
- Cherry, Bekaert & Holland
  One NCNB Plaza
  Charlotte, NC 28280
  (704) 377-1678
- Clifton, Gunderson & Co.
  900 Commercial National Bank
    Building

Peoria, IL 61602
(309) 671-4500
- Coopers & Lybrand
  1251 Avenue of the Americas
  New York, NY 10020
  (212) 536-2000
- Crowe, Chizek
  330 East Jefferson Blvd.
  South Bend, IN 46624
  (219) 232-3992
- Deloitte Haskins & Sells
  1114 Avenue of the Americas
  New York, NY 10036
  (212) 790-0500
- Ernst & Whinney
  200 National City Center
  Cleveland, Ohio 44114
- Grant Thornton
  Prudential Plaza
  Chicago, IL 60601
  (312) 856-0001
- KMG Main Hurdman
  55 East 52nd St.
  New York, NY 10055
  (212) 909-5000
- Laventhol and Horwath
  1845 Walnut St.
  Philadelphia, PA 10103
  (215) 299-1600
- Kenneth Leventhal & Co.
  2049 Century Park East
  Los Angeles, CA 90067
  (213) 277-0880
- Mann Judd Landau
  230 Park Avenue
  New York, NY 10169
  (212) 661-5500
- McGladrey Hendrickson & Pullen
  640 Capital Square
  Des Moines, IA 50309
  (515) 284-8680
- Moss Adams
  2830 Bank of California Center
  Seattle, WA 98164
  (206) 223-1820
- Geo. S. Olive & Co.
  320 North Meridian St.
  Indianapolis, IN 46204
  (317) 267-8400

- Oppenheim, Appel, Dixon & Co.
  101 Park Ave.
  New York, NY 10178
  (212) 422-1000
- Pannell Kerr Forster
  262 North Belt East
  Houston, TX 77060
  (713) 999-5134
- Peat, Marwick Main
  345 Park Ave.
  New York, NY 10022
  (212) 758-9700
- Plante & Moran
  26211 Central Park Blvd.
  Southfield, MI 48037
  (313) 352-2500

- Price Waterhouse & Co.
  1251 Avenue of the Americas
  New York, NY 10020
  (212) 489-8900
- Seidman & Seidman
  15 Columbus Circle
  New York, NY 10023
  (212) 657-7500
- Touche Ross & Co.
  1633 Broadway
  New York, NY 10019
  (212) 489-1600
- Arthur Young & Co.
  277 Park Ave.
  New York, NY 10172
  (212) 407-1500

Source: "Public Accounting Report," an Atlanta-based newsletter that tracks the accounting profession. 404/455-7600

BLUE SKY LISTING: STATE SECURITIES ADMINISTRATORS AND COMMISSIONS OF THE UNITED STATES

Alabama: 166 Constitution Street, Second Floor, Montgomery, AL 36130

Alaska: Division of Banking & Securities, 333 Willoughby Street, P.O. Box D, Juneau, AK 99811

Arizona: 1200 West Washington Street, Phoenix, AZ 85007

Arkansas: 201 East Markham, Third Floor, Little Rock, AR 72201

California: Department of Corporations, 1025 P Street, Suite 205, Sacramento, CA 95814

Colorado: Division of Securities, 1560 Broadway, Suite 1450, Denver, CO 80202

Connecticut: Banking Department, Division of Securities and Business Investments, 44 Capitol Avenue, Hartford, CT 06106

Delaware: Division of Securities, State Office Building, 820 North French Street, 8th floor, Wilmington, DE 19801

District of Columbia: 451 Indiana Avenue, N.W., Suite 323, Washington, DC 20001

Florida: Division of Securities, Department of Banking and Finance, The Capitol, Tallahassee, FL 32301

Georgia: Securities Division, West Tower, 2 Martin Luther King, Jr. Drive, Suite 802, Atlanta, GA 30334

Hawaii: Department of Commerce and Consumer Affairs, 1010 Richards Street, Honolulu, HI 96813

Idaho: Statehouse, Boise, ID 83720

Illinois: Illinois Securities Department, 900 South Spring Street, Springfield, IL 62704

Indiana: One North Capitol, Suite 560, Indianapolis, IN 46204

Iowa: Lucas State Office Building, Des Moines, IA 50319

Kansas: 503 Kansas Avenue, Suite 212, Topeka, KS 66603

Kentucky: 911 Leawood Drive, Frankfort, KY 40601

Louisiana: 315 Louisiana State Office Building, New Orleans, LA 70112
Maine: State House Station 36, Augusta, ME 04333
Maryland: Munsey Building, 4th floor, 7 North Calvert Street, Baltimore, MD 21202
Massachusetts: The Commonwealth of Massachusetts, Secretary of the Commonwealth, Securities Division, John W. McCormack Building, Room 1719, One Ashburton Place, Boston, MA 02108
Michigan: Corporation & securities Bureau, Department of Commerce, P.O. Box 30222, 6546 Mercantile Way, Lansing, MI 48909
Minnesota: 500 Metro Square Building, St. Paul, MN 55101
Mississippi: 401 Mississippi Street, P.O. Box 136, Jackson, MS 39205
Missouri: Harry S. Truman Office Building, Jefferson City, MO 65102
Montana: Office of the State Auditor, Securities Department, P.O. Box 4009, Helena, MT 59604
Nebraska: 301 Centennial Mall South, P.O. Box 95006, Lincoln, NE 68509-5006
Nevada: State Capitol, Carson City, NV 89710
New Hampshire: 169 Manchester Street, Concord, NH 03301
New Jersey: 80 Mulberry Street, Room 308, Newark, NJ 07102
New Mexico: Securities Division, Lew Wallace Building, Santa Fe, NM 87503
New York: Two World Trade Center, New York, NY 10047
North Carolina: Office of the Secretary of State, Securities Division, 300 North Salisbury St., Room 302, Raleigh, NC 27611
North Dakota: State Capitol, Bismarck, ND 58505
Ohio: Two Nationwide Plaza, Columbus, OH 43215
Oklahoma: Securities Commission, 2915 North Lincoln, Oklahoma City, OK 73105
Oregon: Department of Commerce, Corporation Division, 1580-12th Street N.E., Salem, OR 97310
Pennsylvania: 333 Market Street, Harrisburg, PA 17101
Puerto Rico: Department of Treasury, P.O. Box 2-4515. San Juan, Puerto Rico 00905
Rhode Island: 100 North Main Street, Providence, RI 02903
South Carolina: 816 Keenan Building, Columbia, SC 29201
South Dakota: 910 E. Sioux, Pierre, SC 57501
Tennessee: Department of Commerce & Insurance, Securities Division, 1808 West End Building, Nashville, TN 37219
Texas: Box 13167, Capitol Station, Austin, TX 78711-3167
Utah: Heber M. Wells Building, 160 E. 300 South, Saalt Lake City, UT 84111
Vermont: State Office Building, Montpelier, VT 05602
Virginia: 11 South 12th Street, Richmond, VA 23219
Washington: Securities Division, Business and Professions Administration, P.O. Box 648, Olympia, WA 98504
West Virginia: Room 118-W, State Capitol Building, Charleston, WV 25305
Wisconsin: P.O. Box 1768, Madison, WI 53701
Wyoming: State Capitol Building, Cheyenne, WY 82002-0020

Bibliography

Blackman, Irving L. *The Valuation of Privately-Held Businesses.* Chicago, IL: Probus Publishing Co., 1986.

Bower, Joseph L. *When Markets Quake.* Cambridge, MA: Harvard Business School Press, 1986.

Childe, John F. *Corporate Finance and Capital Management for the Chief Executive Officer and Directors.* Englewood Cliffs, NJ: Prentice-Hall, 1979.

Cross, Thomas B. *Knowledge Engineering.* New York: Simon & Schuster, 1988.

Davis, F. T., Jr. *Business Acquisitions Desk Book.* Institute for Business Planning, 1977.

Downes, John, and Jordan Elliot Goodman. *Barron's Finance and Investment Handbook.* New York: Barron's Educational Series, Inc., 1986.

Heskett, James L. *Managing in the Service Economy.* Cambridge, MA: Harvard Business School Press, 1986.

Kaufman, Henry. *Interest Rates, the Markets, and the New Financial World.* New York: Times Books, 1986.

Lee, Steven James, and Robert Douglas Colman, (Eds.). *Handbook of Mergers, Acquisitions and Buyouts.* Englewood Cliffs, NJ: Prentice-Hall, 1981.

Lindsey, Jennifer. *The Entrepreneur's Guide to Capital.* Chicago, IL: Probus Publishing Co., 1986.

Peters, Tom. *Thriving on Chaos.* New York: Alfred A. Knopf, 1987.

Purcell, W. R. Jr. *Understanding a Company's Finances.* Boston: Houghton Mifflin Company, 1981.

Silver, A. David. *The Silver Prescription.* NewYork: John Wiley & Sons, 1987.

INDEX